# Reinventing Leadership

By

Paul T. Thomas

LLYFRAU
CAMBRIA

Published in the United Kingdom in 2014 by
Cambria Books, Wales, United Kingdom

# Acknowledgements

Rhian, Saffir and Bronwen must, of course, as family, take centre stage in the completion of this work. Simply to say a very big thank you for their support and sorry for not being there when it mattered. I would ask forgiveness for all the school events I've missed and the day to day family life as a result of this passion to democratise the workplace, which has taken me, if not in body away from the home, but in soul when I've sat there many a night typing away pretending to listen (which I'm sure I never really got away with ...).

I have to start firstly by thanking all those people I have had contact with in and out of the workplace, such as Mr Mike Sheppard, my old PE teacher, who taught me the value of sport in building life confidence. It's strange to start with your PE teacher, but Mike was able, through canoeing, climbing and mountaineering, to build a confidence in me when others simply dismissed. He was the first teacher, along with Mr White (Physics) that had a real passion for teaching and their subjects, and it rubbed off. It's the passion in something that counts.

I must also mention Philip Catherwood at the Welsh Government who helped the DNA project with his detailed mindset and goal of perfection, and Prof Alan Lovell, without whose support and trust I would certainly not be the person I am today. Indeed. Prof Lovell was, as Dean, one of the most human, trustworthy, passionate and loyal academics I have ever experienced. Indeed, since his retirement I have never found such a person in the academic profession since, but still live in hope.

Also, my time, mind and life would not be what they are today if it were not for Kelly Page, an Australian with a Welsh mindset. Passionate, thorough, and an academic who is not only brilliant in her field but interested in making the world a better place by rigorous, valid research. I spent many an hour picking up the pieces of broken thoughts and ideas after Kelly first questioned them and then tore them apart in the early days of this movement. The experience was painful, but much better than going foolishly into the 'silly zone' (real companies) without a real question to explore. As she says, the question is far more important than the answer.

I must also thank Andy McCann, one of those rare people in life that have the same qualities and values in life as myself. Never once has he asked, 'how much money is there?' in any of our projects or speaker events. Never has there been a question on why we are doing it, it's simply a given.

Philip Crocker, an MBA graduate at Glamorgan, a true gentleman and fantastic wingman in any situation. Strong core values and a passion for people. John Batten, a colleague at Glamorgan University as was a true, open, hard speaking academic who's real world experience made him an instant enemy of the charlatans who professed worldly knowledge in business from books and research.

John Ward, who I have mentioned throughout and who has helped co-authored a section, is also a person who 'got-it' at MBA teaching and then used 'it' back in his company with mixed reviews. I always remember him saying, 'If I die with money in my pocket I will be disappointed.' His zest for life is truly amazing even at the age of sixty (ha ha, joke... he's seventy-five really).

Chay Billen needs another massive thank you, not only for the fact that he's a massive bloke, a walking 6'6" muscleman, but because he has also kept me sane over the past fifteen years as a training partner, fitness guru, and all-round top-bloke, and he is someone with extremely set core values.

I cannot, nor will ever forget the work of Gemma Collins, whose writing and production of the BBC Radio and TV documentaries is littered throughout this book. Without her intellect, organisation and belief most of this would not have been written. The opposite of Chay above, in that she is tiny in stature, has hair and, well, isn't a bloke, but her energy, leadership and outputs are the same.

My final note must be to my parents, Terry and Lorraine Thomas. They have always been there in times of trouble, failure and missing issues without questions or judgement. Indeed, if it wasn't for my mother's attitude in times of good and bad I would have crumbled a long time ago. Sadly, for me and the world, she passed away on 13th Feb 2012, the day of my birth. We will all miss her Welsh cakes, cooked Sunday dinner, and direct comments of truth in moments of difficulty.

Dr Paul.... The main culprit
*(I know that's nothing like me but shhhh don't tell him)*

Artwork by Romano Marenghi
*(I know it's nothing like him, but have you seen Paul in real life!....)*

*"Simplexity: the art of
making the complex simple"*
Dr Paul Thomas

# Contents

# The Author

**Doctor Paul Thomas is known by the BBC as the 'Business Doctor' and is an experienced and respected voice on matters relating to change, leadership, organisational development and structures that allow people to thrive and flourish within organisations.**

He works with private and public sector organisations of all sizes, including multi-nationals, showing them there are effective ways to run the workplace, which increase outcomes and service effectiveness without losing front-line staff. Don't call him a consultant or academic! He firmly believes that most consultants will try to impose their own solutions on a company, whilst academics prefer theory rather than actual practice change. He believes in unlocking the potential of the staff to solve the problems themselves. Paul's dislike of management practices is nothing personal – he just thinks the way most businesses are managed is out dated.

Paul is the former Head of Leadership at Glamorgan Business School, Leadership Fellow at Sheffield Hallam University and is currently Hon. Fellow at Plymouth

University. He is founder and co-Director of DNA Definitive and his work has taken him to India, China, Pakistan, Dubai, the USA and many European countries. He completed a global action research project on leadership and complexity thinking, visiting nineteen countries in six months and has continued to change leadership practices in small, medium and large companies for over 20 years. Paul left University life to focus completely on his theory as practice of organisational life, leadership and frontline engagement.

Paul is a fascinating and impressive business speaker whose insight is in high demand throughout the business world.

## What People Say:

*"Paul's ideas on management are inspirational and thought-provoking. They may appear radical and revolutionary but they're not, simply because they are actually so intuitive and common-sensical. Paul is also quite possibly the most engaging speaker I've heard in a long time.*

*Any manager - or leader - who wants to get the most out of their organisation really should consider talking to Paul."*

Gemma Collins, Producer, BBC News.

*"Since the 1990's, I've worked with some of the best people and organizations -- Santa Fe Institute, MIT, National Defense University, Alidade Institute -- on translating the sciences of complexity into practical leadership for military and civilian organizations. Paul's deep insights, boundless energy, warm sense of humour make him among the top 3 breakthrough leaders I have met and worked with throughout my military and civilian career."*

Dan Moore Director, International Air Defence, Raytheon Missile Systems.

*"Paul's depth understanding of traditional management practices is more than matched by his desire to do something about them and create a more human centred and effective approach to running our businesses.*

*Paul brings expertise in the application of Complexity sciences to understanding how our organisations (don't) work and the often surprisingly simple solutions to our everyday problems that plague organisational life.*

*I have engaged Paul to work with me on several occasions either consulting on specific issues or to give talks to members of the management population on a Complex Adaptive Systems outlook on life in organisations. He has never failed to deliver real world solutions that actually work and I look forward to working with him again."*

Mick Rogers Operations Director, Airbus UK.

*"I made an hour long BBC documentary following Paul's work in the Environmental Services Department of Blaenau Gwent Council. This gave me a unique insight into his working methods and the results achieved.*

*He led an impressive project over four months creating a framework in which front-line staff took on management responsibilities, with great success. It was extremely labour-intensive and Paul never failed to put in the gruelling hours required.*

*The results were outstanding - increased efficiency, savings, streamlined management, and a genuinely more empowered workforce. Impressive stuff."*

Deborah Perkin Senior Producer, BBC.

*"Dr Paul Thomas is a force of nature! Some time ago, I ran a seminar on leadership and management for the incubating businesses, and invited them to bring their clients along. Paul's ideas are, to put it mildly, revolutionary in a world that looks for certain well-recognised pathways to success, and is constantly 'tweaking' them. This session was the liveliest we have ever run; interactive just about describes it!*

*If you want to provoke thought, debate, action and reaction, Paul Thomas will lead you into new territory. Enjoy!"*

Pam Voisey Business Incubation Manager, University of South Wales.

4

# My Journey – The Beginning

*'[One cannot] predict future events exactly if one cannot even measure the present state of the universe precisely.'* *(Hawking, 2002: 5)*

When I began this journey in 1998, I had no idea of the effect that this work would have on me, why would I, but the reality, luck and lessons learned have been truly amazing. It has impacted not only my professional career as a former manager, academic and now author, but has also had an effect on my personal life and on my friendships. Its for this reason alone I want to share some of the inspirational stories of change, challenge and passions that just happen to be in the world of business. So this book contains business, methods, and tool here and there, and a little advise, but please remember I'm not right, I certainly don't wish you to repeat my journey, but more than anything I want you to take confidence in what you are doing is fine, and if not the helpful hints in here to go off and do it your way.

I look back to the catalyst for this book and many of my writings and teaching for that matter. Sheffield Hallam University in 1995, where I first registered my interest in doing a PhD, I remember the problems I was having with supervisors who disappeared through retirement or ill health and the disruption to continuity that resulted. It was without question a miserable experience, one that helped form my supervision skills later on in my career as an academic PhD Director of Studies for PhD & DBA, in how 'not to do it'. I also remember the contrast in my subsequent discovery of two passionate, patient, and committed academics at Keele University, Professor Miriam David, and Dr Stephen Whitehead, who were willing to corral my energy and efforts into this text and help me to become much more academic.

They 'showed' me how to think critically about the status quo, always to question and, more importantly, not to worry too much about the impression those questions made! That may seem a strange thing to say, but often to question was to be seen to have an 'attitude' or to have a 'chip on your shoulder' or worse still to be seen as just plain awkward. I am, still, proud of being awkward, but hopefully in a questioning way, in the way people expect an 'academic' to question. However, I'm also sure that the so-called academics who are more like bureaucrats that have infiltrated the upper sanctum of the schools, would sharply disagree, but more on that later.

I have to say that being in the world of academia, or indeed outside looking in, venturing in only when it suits me, I am becoming increasing uncomfortable with the general lack of questioning there is today, and which has steadily declined since 1998. Instead we seem to be encouraging a new breed of 'smart administrators' rather than classical academic thinkers. Lecturers often seem more comfortable teaching from core text on a multitude of subjects, none of which they research or, dare I say, are interested in, and who subscribe to the concept of students as customers. I know this is a hugely controversial statement, one which will upset many of my former colleagues, but this is something I'm not unknown for saying. Indeed, after saying this very thing on a BBC documentary in 2012, I was asked to leave one Business School Campus in South Wales, UK, by the then new Dean with whom I worked with in Glamorgan for being too controversial, even though I was only having a coffee with the Associate Dean, who, in my defence, invited me in for a chat. I still use that story as evidence of the problems in Business Schools and organisations in general. This is where ego takes over from

learning and co-evolution. I still today learn far more from my detractors than I do from like minded friends/colleagues.

So this work began in the true sense for me in 1999 when the University of Wales began operating an overseas collaboration with Hainan University in China to deliver the MBA programme, although the grounding was way back in the 70's growing up in a mining and steel working community in the South Wales Valleys. The programme was originally designed by Harvard Business School, and is allegedly aimed at high-level management and senior executives. Mintzberg (2004) succinctly defines the MBA as an attempt to educate managers to think at a strategic level of organisational development, in the context of human interaction and connectivity, to create wealth for the 'owners'. The programme structure at the beginning of our teaching of the MBA in China and in Wales followed the classical routes in modules leading from such areas as Finance to final modules such as Strategic Planning.

In May 2000 I was one of a team of three academics based at the University of Wales, Newport, who ventured into the Chinese business world to teach the final stages of the award, set at Masters Level 7.

The initial stages 1 and 2 (level 5 & 6), include Accounts, Statistics, Marketing etc. and were taught by the Professors of Hainan and other visiting professors from universities around China, using materials provided by UK based academics in Newport. Once the students had 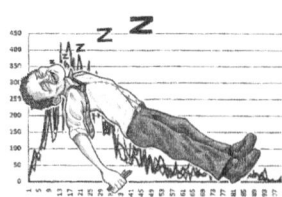 completed the first stages successfully (moderated throughout by the University of Wales team), I would then teach the final stage 7 (Masters level) modules of Strategy and Innovation prior to the students beginning their research dissertations.

A small side story – when I first visited China, I was warned about 'saving face', which is a term used to describe how not to offend the Chinese, and more importantly to allow them room to manoeuvre if things go wrong, or there is a failure on their part. Whilst this was worrying at the time I quickly learned in the four years teaching there that this was in part nonsense, and only really meant for those in the 'trusted network' or guanxi (more on this later). However on my first visit, I was given the task to review, check, moderate and comment on some forty completed MBA dissertations … overnight!

Now after a journey of nineteen hours, most of which was spent in 'cattle class', I wasn't best placed for such a task, especially given that any review of a MBA dissertation would normally mean at least two to three hours work. Anyhow, the jet-lag set in, so sleep was not an issue and I cracked on with the marking. By morning I had managed to sample almost 70 per cent of the marked dissertations and quickly realised that no-one in the forty strong cohort had failed, and they all had marks of 70 per cent upwards.

This is where I am sure my former MBA students will be gripping the side of this book or kindle about to shout. This type of individual score and grade in most Masters is difficult. To achieve a group pass rate of 100 per cent is impossible. Indeed, I used to warn my students that only 30 per cent who started the MBA would actually achieve a successful outcome. Changing jobs, getting married or divorced, or both, losing interest and, of course, failing one of the twelve modules, were all obstacles that would claim their victims along the way.

So, there was an immediate problem. Apart from the fact that the Chinese academics were unfamiliar with the UK standards and expectations, the dissertations themselves were pretty basic ... okay, they were awful. There was, however, one much bigger issue. I was the one about to tell thirty senior Chinese academics that their students were not graduating today as I was failing all forty dissertations, the final capstone of the MBA assessment scheme.

That takes me back to the 'trusted relationships' and 'saving face'. How on earth was I going to tell them and allow them to save face, when clearly there was no wriggle room? My colleagues sat either side of me, unaware of the doom and shame I was about to unleash. Chairing the Board was Huw Williams, who was the most ethical, moral and quality driven Deputy Dean I have ever had the pleasure of working with. He leant over and simply whispered 'standards must be maintained regardless', which was my cue to grow in confidence.

The Board started as normal, with all the representatives, academics and Vice Chancellor from the Chinese University introducing themselves ... no, wait! Vice Chancellor of the

University? Oh bloody hell; they have only brought in the main person to celebrate the first western cohort passing their MBA in China! My confidence disappeared, and sleep deprivation kicked in. I was completely lost for words; I stuttered, muttered and wished for a hole to appear and swallow me up so that I could escape from the meeting of doom. I did not dare to look up, but I stole a quick glance and I noticed the Chinese VC who burped and then slowly picked his nose before examining the contents trapped in his nail.

My colleague, Kath, also saw this and began to giggle quietly next to me. This was the butterfly effect in action for sure, and never have I seen a better example. The sleep deprivation, stress and fear were immediately replaced with giggles from me this time, our heads down as we regressed into five year old status. Poor old Huw Williams tried to carry on, but then simply called for a refreshment break. He then took me aside and told me off in no uncertain terms, I pulled myself together and delivered the doom to a less than supportive audience. I survived, but they never gave me the MBA dissertations to validate again. Nor did I ever see the nose-picking VC again.

*Anyhow, sorry, back to the book ...*

The MBA and university education seems to be a critical issue for managers and for any prospect of progress in managerial careers both in China and in the UK (Keown, 1986; Venter, 2000; Lee, 2003). Indeed, after the Chinese government closed universities in the 1980s and early 1990s, many students saw education as a much lamented and important 'missing' part of their lives as they realised that they were not going to be able to attend university as they could have done twenty years earlier.

There are still more men than women currently on higher educational programmes although women are increasingly entering fields of study previously deemed to be the preserve of the male student by Chinese society (Lee, 2004).

Women studying at Hainan University, for instance, made up more than 40 per cent of the business and economics degree student body in 2000.  This rose to 51 per cent by 2005, a factor that reflects current trends in China (Asia Economic Press 2005). According to Jing (2001: 104), the education profile of women managers is now similar to that of male managers. The Times newspaper, reporting on modern China, stated that over 45 per cent of all young females (24–35 years old) were now wealthy, educated and managing their own organisations.

Women managers are making inroads into the top of organisational hierarchies, but these still tend to be in areas considered extensions of the kinds of roles that women would traditionally play within the family.

It is almost twenty years since the term 'glass ceiling' was used in the Wall Street Journal to describe the specious barriers that prevent women from reaching top levels of organisational management. Whilst several governments, including those in the USA, the UK and China, have developed special committees to remove barriers to women's participation, research by the Economist confirms a global down shift of 0.7 per cent in women's participation at executive level within organisations. Europe and the USA each have only 4.6 per cent of women at senior executive level (2010) and this is a downward trend not an improving picture, as most people might expect.

According to Canfield University Business School at the time (Welks, 2004), the number of female executive directors of FT-SE 100 companies rose from eleven in 2000 to seventeen in 2004. This means seventeen women against a number of almost four hundred men.

No British woman has to date headed a blue chip British company, yet 44 per cent of the workforce is female. The Economist attempts to explain why women fail to reach executive level within organisations. It states that many firms still have a culture of sport related discourse and late-night drinking to 'oil the wheels'. It also comments on the pervasive stereotyping of women's capacity for leadership.

This was, when I look back, the revelation that began my journey. I wanted to know why these women were in positions of management at all, given the adverse statistics of male/female owner-managers in China and the rest of the world. I was astonished to realise that anyone who did not conform to the aggressive, strong, masculine norm was automatically considered inadequate (much more on this later).

When I began teaching in 1995 I came to it from twelve years in public and private sector management and I did not, to any real extent, question the social and organisational world around me.

The practice of looking, speaking, writing and thinking involves learning to interpret and to think about relationships of power and influence. Bourdieu (2005:21), whose work I read in a moment of boredom, (and I'm so glad I did) comments that the purpose of research and questioning is not to gather information about how society is organised, but rather to critique the practices and discourses that stand as truths for us. Yet since starting my quest to rid the world of the thing we call management, I understand increasingly clearly that we live in cultures and tribes that are constantly infiltrated by visual images, signals, responses and purposes that have various intended and unintended effects on what we do and how we think. I have also realised that we accept these intrusions into our consciousness, largely without question. This refers not only to the use of language but also to images that convey their own meaning.

I was most aware of this when I was working away from my own culture and the language I know well, when I was in China, teaching, for instance. I had naïvely taken for granted the language we use to understand, describe, and define the world around us. A language like English has set rules defining the way we express and interpret meaning. Systems of representations of action, photography, and text have this function as well.

I partially support as a result the view of Lingard et al (2003) that suggests that we construct our world and its meaning through these systems of representation. However, assumptions that the individual is constituted automatically by systems of representation do not fully explain the reality, power, or agency of the individual. When I was in China, or in India for that matter, I began to think about these systems of representation and to understand how we construct the meaning of the world and the organisations around us. What I had, up to this point, understood to be management and organisation, I began now to see as constructs that are represented through both theory and in discourse itself. To put it simply, we kind of made it up depending on our culture, education and context! This realisation made me want to dig deeper; who made it up, and for what purpose?

This kind of construction is formed from the rules and conventions of the system in which we find ourselves, which I now understand to be, in simple terms, culture. Yet, for my students on the MBA journey, this mind-set was being expanded by globalisation and the arrival of western teaching and professional business educators.

What did I, for example, as a male 'teacher' and 'business strategist' entering the Chinese business world, represent? Did I help anyone? I mean did anyone actually improve their business or career as a result of the teachings rather than the award itself?

Whilst teaching managers I also became aware of the possible impact I would have as a teacher who advocated 'Western traditional, rational, reductionist management' literature to a growing economy. Was I helping these managers to become leaders? Did I help the managers understand that everyone could play an important part in the creation of a successful organisation? Or was I reinforcing the concept of male supremacy and the 'one way of doing business'? Was I simply naively bolstering the status quo, which kept the workers in their place and the managers in power?

At this point I cannot avoid mentioning the undermining of taken-for-granted beliefs. For a number of years I have felt that whilst I am better off now in material terms than I was ten years ago, there is still something lacking in my life and the

14

lives of people in the West (de-Botten, 2009). We have more and more choices in what we do, what we consume, and how we live our lives, but this seems to make life more difficult rather than easier.

Globalisation has continued to create ever increasing bewilderment and the world is still confused by what we have created, particularly where our work and our organisations are concerned.

During my work as a Manager and Academic, which I will detail promise, I continued to question my own actions and the effect I had on the world around me. My doubts arose from realising that, as I was a man, I was the beneficiary of a belief system that undermined and altered the lives of others simply through perpetuated deep-rooted assumptions. The notion of Simplexity which I talk about throughout this work, is simply about making the complex-simple, and moves the organisation away from Managerialism and into the notions of democratic, consensual leadership (Weber & Thomas 2013) focused on the value added to service output and notion of effective over efficient. Applying Simplexity as a multi-methods architecture as I will detail at the end of the book, is an extension of Complex Evolving Systems (Milton-Kelly 2004/08, McMillian 2010, Thomas 2014) the concept of *knowledge-power*, change, Leadership, and the relationship between frontline and leadership, can all be influenced and influences the adaptive and innovative practice of people, in a positive way, by naturally generating negotiation that accommodates a diversity of worldviews – 'IF' the purpose of what they are there for is clear. Organisations are within Simplexity; human, complex (and I don't mean complicated) and fundamentally different from machine-type systems and therefore 'management'. Accordingly, human behaviour is not therefore fully predictable and people are capable of changing their rules of interaction, thus changing expected outcomes. Staff are able to *self-organise*, to influence each other and be influenced in turn, and this reciprocal influence can change ideas, behaviour, ways of thinking, mindsets, working and relating on the micro-levels in which the impact is seen only way down the 'system' timeline - that is, humans are able to *co-evolve*, to self-organise and to *create something new that is emergent* in the sense that it could not have been predicted at the outset. People, and staff create intricate *networks of relationships* sustained through communication and other forms of *feedback, which is called shadow-systems (Stacey 2004)*, with varying degrees of *inter-dependence*. Although heavily influenced by their history, education, context and culture they can transcend all when necessary as evidenced in the two case studies. When they meet a rule that doesn't suit most are able to explore the *space of possibilities* and find a different way of doing things, i.e. they are creative and innovative. Extending the idea of the appeal to leadership as a form of identity manipulation and co-option, I point out later on how some senior managers, civil servants, Heads of School and Social Workers, are usually relatively skeptical of notions of management, and have been more susceptible to taking a 'leadership role' in promoting changes.  Yet, whilst the word manager is exchanged for leader, the behavior unfortunately doesn't at least in the longer term.

The patterning is not fixed in these case stories which I tell throughout the book, but fractal, as diverse claims to the truth attempt to reconstitute the dominant claims of the context, naturally influencing and adapting practice that is service led/driven, even my own. It is the power innate in this co-evolutionary behaviour that becomes the vital dynamic of the change and leadership practice, because in each local context it is the essential stimulus that ensures the system can transform its own functioning in a legitimised way.

However attempts to fix the direction of power and to control agent/staff behaviour through the discourses of rules, policy and controls can easily remove the tension or stimulus needed for a system to negotiate new practice. Whilst there is little argument with the need to minimise costs the norms conveyed by managerialism in any context or sector, the traditional notions of 'management' counter the autonomy and self-regulatory capacity of professionals by challenging and redefining the orientation of frontline line service reality. Simplexity Leadership is an architecture designed to help processes through robust organic methods of change, regulation, such as peer coaching, trust and risk, establishing a set of discourses that legitimate non-normalisation, non-hierarchical observation and examination in a way that runs parallel to leadership, creating strong notions of self regulation, creativity, fun, freedom and self-mastery.

So as I examined my work life experience, and with some relevant reading, I quickly began to understand that forces, which we cannot harness and that are possibly beyond our control, shape us. I began to see that the beliefs, which had always given me such certainty and comfort, and had promoted the idea that if you keep to the rules and trust in superior power all will be well, were actually false. I began to doubt that the management and organisational theory I had learned, had applied, and that I now taught to virgin MBA'ers and MSc'ers, actually reflected reality. As a result of these doubts I began to question my own understanding of the role of management in organisations and, indeed, my own role as a former manager and teacher. I soon realised that the theory I had learned did not truly reflect my experience. I had been unable, in the past, to express this view freely for fear of being seen as different or, worse still, as not being 'management material' and miss all (other) promotions to the upper-sanctums. I have to say that having spent a short time as Head of Leadership, even this experience made me realise that I was not 'cut from the same cloth' as most on the Senior Management Teams. I found most to be devoid of emotional intelligence, passion for the service and the rare few, integrity.

Paradoxically, at that same moment (although this was not linear or time bound), I understood that we couldn't escape the interconnectedness of our social world. The subsequent development of our actions in relation to others' will alter when we are caught, even very slightly, between two worlds. This was very true for me as an educator, teaching groups of up to fifty senior business people every six to eight weeks, all of whom needed and demanded 'facts' and answers (also supported by Connell, 1995 and Mintzberg, 2004). To which sadly and to my dying shame I provided in buckets loads.

I soon found out that 'beliefs begin when facts run-out' (Handy, 1992:79). The realisation that no individual can prove that their own beliefs are correct to any other individual led to a significant change in my own thought processes. This knowledge captured a lot of the issues I had when I was teaching the MBA. This knowledge also brought with it a confidence in what I thought and believed and with this came an acceptance of what others thought and believed, without reliance on supporting facts or statistics. It was liberating to realise that facts do not necessarily provide the answer. Conversely, being certain about something does not condemn any thinking or research to a rational reductionist scientific critique.

This is my journey, my research, and my quest to change organisations to face the realities of being human, messy and therefore to perhaps learn a new game, the game of nature and natural systems. The premises and work here represent my opinions, backed up with 'real' evidence, both substantiated and anecdotal. The dogged reliance on facts and figures is something that constantly amuses me at academic conferences and this is not a work that would delight a quantitative statistician or even get him or her mildly excited about its numbers and facts. But it will, I believe, be the beginning of a revolution in our traditional understanding of what management is and what it does, and more importantly why it must be removed from organisational life.

So let me warn you (again)... this is NOT a business or for that matter an academic book. Apart from the last few chapters, there isn't much of a structure, let alone a model, formulae or theory that you can subtract and apply to your world. I make no apology for this, for having read far too many academic and business books, I feel almost overdosed by the quest of many to prove, justify, construct a view of the world of business, so we can manage, control and predict the future. I'm just not having any of it, including conforming to the genre of business books, or formulaic structure. You'll pick up the reason for this quite quickly in this book as your read on. But this book is about how someone like me, did things in business and academia to help change the world a little, all from a Complexity Theory perspective and absolute standpoint, without constantly referring back to this architecture, in a way that so simple. Why? Well I always felt my role as manager and academic, was to make things simple and fun. To remove the fear of moving away from the traditional model and mindset of organisations to something, a little more human, messy and exciting. So this book is the history of impact of what changed me as a business person, why it impacted the way it did, so you can realise how great you are as a change agent, with the opportunity to change the miserable world of work in which we lose so much of our life. Oh.. and make you a little bit curious...

# Chapter 1
# It's the 21st Century, Stop Managing People!

It's a simply statement to say that the majority of people in industry are hard working, loyal, innovative, creative, passionate and committed – except for the eight hours when they are at work! It seems that all those great qualities, disappears as soon as they enter the workplace, because when they are in work they have to be supervised, controlled, monitored, measured and told what to do by means of myriad rules, regulations, procedures and policies. Why?

The problem does not lie with the fitter, teacher, Social Workers or the receptionist, as most managers might think, it lies with the notion and mindset of managers, of management itself; the endless systems, processes and structures and their need to control the how, not just why things are done.

Disagree? Then just ask your workers if they are excited about coming to work each day. Then ask your managers the same question and you'll probably get a very different response. Indeed, working for the past tens years in academia I've experienced a fair share of line-managers who, and I wish I had a dollar for every time I heard it, say, 'Yes, I know it doesn't work, but it's the process,' or, 'We have to do it this way as it's the system.'

The majority of managers, team leaders and supervisors know that the system, rules, processes and procedures are wrong and don't help. For whatever reason they cannot or will not amend, alter, bypass or destroy, instead waiting for some magic 'anti-daft process fairy' to miracle up a new, common sense way and rescue them from the mad management virus.

Writing in some editions of various professional journals, I have always attempted to explore and explain why the role of 'manager' is dead, along with the notions of planning, control and structure in any industry. I felt it was important to be that blunt. I wanted no misunderstanding around the notion of playing with words or moving terms academically from 'manager' to 'leader' and such like. There is a Russian saying that the 'fish rots from the head', and in the case of management in the 21st century, it is not only rotting, it's now beginning to smell quite badly!

Those of you that were around in the 80's and 90's will be able to remember the revolution that took place amongst frontline workers and the 'shift of power' in the unions. Now, however, revolution must be in the boardroom, and within the ranks of senior managers, the way they operate and of course the gender. Many companies around the world are already running without managers, indeed some companies like Nucor Steel, USA, a Fortune 500 company which has 48,000 workers, are already reaping the benefits.

To survive as a sustainable culture and industry on a local, national and international scale, managing with 19th

Century principles and thinking has to stop and the industry will have to make the leap to the 21st Century.

In this, my first book, I put forward the need for change and why this change was needed in the 'management' field. DNA Definitive/UK, founded in 2003, is a collaborative network with key economy enhancing bodies such as industry associations, private enterprise, higher education and government. I had always argued as part of the DNA group, that we must encourage and support managers to become critical about managerial thinking and practice because, for the most part, managing today just doesn't stack up.

Managers or should I say 'management', the thing we do, rather than the people, tends to treat people like children, telling them when to come in, what to do, even, at times, requiring them to ask permission to go to the toilet!  Then, of course, allowing them to go home at a certain time. The problem with this is that if adults are treated like children they will act like children. We need to stop 'buying' the time of people in companies, and concentrate on buying talent.  Many people working already see themselves working as a vocation – a lifestyle that they are passionate about. These are people who have talent and people skills, and are unspoilt by the notions of conforming to out-dated principles such as management.

You only have to look at the creative industries, such as fashion or design to see what difference there is in how people are treated. I know here, there is the argument that this is a different context, what about the binman or factory worker. They need managing, surely? Well no, to be honest. Just because you or I think the job is repugnant, awful, too hard, or just plainly beneath us as we have 'qualifications' or 'I went to school' as one Leisure Manager stated as a defence, that does not justify treating them like children. Indeed, throughout the past 17 years working in over 100 differing organisations, the most clear fact was that the binmen, like other frontline workers were proud of what they accomplished each day, had pride just like the Surgeon, the Teacher, or Minister.

We tend to do jobs (if allowed) that really interest us. If we do a job that interests us, then the passion (energy) to make a difference is innate. So we should be employing talent seekers not HR Managers, so they can grow this passion not enforce out of date, energy sapping rules, policies and procedures. We should have talent keepers, not team leaders, or supervisors. Only when we change these titles do we start to see the real roles leaders at all levels play in a successful company or organisation. This isn't a softer form of management or for that matter leadership. The hard discussions which I've not seen happen in organisations with poorly performing people, happens much easier if its about the talent and purpose, not the person, or personal.

When we start to question how managers at all levels manage, the task of removing the traditional 'role' of manager – (again not necessarily the person but the role) – can become extremely contentious. This depth of critical thinking causes uncertainty, fear and worry for most managers. They quickly realise when they question their managerial role that they are not necessarily adding value to the 'customer', but simply creating more bureaucracy, rules and procedures, which can be counter-productive, and cost time and money. Organisational success is about leading the people, not about the systems or processes. They simply support the people to do a super job. If the process, system or form is not adding value then it's a wasteful cost in terms of the company reputation, service and sustainability.

I feel I should say at this point that DNA is not a consultancy, nor am I a consultant. I do not offer 'solutions' or answers, or even a new model for doing things. Consultants are for the most part a symptom of all things wrong with management. They offer what managers want, a simple solution, which is normally counter-intuitive, in that it creates additional problems elsewhere in the organisation and by the way rarely solves the problem at hand, and even the small changes offered are gleaned from the internal staff first. Then more external consultancy is needed to help solve these 'new' problems, and so the spiral begins.

My function is merely to remove the notion that management is led from the top-down, and that decision makers can only be 'managers,' that solutions are singular and simplistic, indeed once the 'solutions' have been found they change during implementation, and finally to illustrate that all situations are created in messy, non-linear, human thinking, which is subjective and constantly changing. It's life! It's nonsense to read or hear that for an organisation to be successful it has to have a good manager – usually male (another argument, for another time!) – at the head of its structure. Actually, the evidence suggests that over the past twenty years, organisations have been successful despite, not because of their management, their systems, planning, and strategising!

So why don't we offer solutions? What is the point of democratising the workforce? Why should you read further? To quote an illustrious Meercat – simples! (I'm sure my international readers would be confused by this, but the Meercat is a commercial in the UK, which lets say caught on)

The solution to every problem will already be within your organisation. It's called your 'frontline staff' and the future is 'engagement'. They are your 'consultants': ready, willing, passionate and, hopefully, loyal to the cause. That's if you allow them to say what they think, encourage debate, trust their opinion, and gain their trust in you.

Management now actively encourages risk aversion. It also demands conformity. Both these issues eliminate diversity, criticality and creativity. Additionally, as we have seen in twenty-three companies from around the world, the more management you have, the slower the company is to react to customer needs and the more dissatisfaction there is amongst frontline employees. Employees feel disempowered and high levels of sickness and absenteeism typically result.

'Management' cannot cope with people who answer back or innovate around 'rules' to achieve greater outputs. One public sector employee described himself as the 'Duracell Bunny' as seen on TV adverts and added, 'When I started I was qualified, passionate and driven to delight customers. I quickly realised that my enthusiasm was not what was required. All management wanted was for me to conform to the rules and procedures – stand on point x until they tell you it's okay to move, etc. My energy quickly left me. Now I just turn-up and wait to be told what to do.'

This is an excellent example of why management in its whole sense must be removed. Management is about power, money and status. There are no other reasons for you to want to become a manager. Now this is where most managers get really angry, and put forward all sorts of reasons why this is incorrect. They give alternative reasons for wanting to become a manager, such as having the freedom to make a difference at work – but even that seemingly laudable ambition is still about power!

Some managers would argue that their staff get more money than they do, but this is only possible if staff work overtime and long hours, so that is not an even playing field! Others say it's not about the status,  so we get managers to remove their shirts and ties, dress the same as frontline workers and get paid the same rate. True democracy only happens when frontline staff are able to vote-in a 'manager', and then, if they are not helping deliver added value to the service, are able to vote them out. Indeed by being on the same rate as frontline workers, the really good, respected, trusted leaders step forward. This, then, is already increasing our ability to serve customers, clients and staff.

To question the managerial practice of the traditional 'command and control process' and consider alternative approaches is of course difficult and challenging in any industry, and there is no guarantee of success. However, the analogy we often use at DNA is that of 'flocking birds'. Flocks of birds operate in a complex, adaptive system, in which there is not just one pair of eyes – the manager looking at the prey, or competition, and searching for food – but a thousand pairs of eyes, with all employees in the organisation searching for the competition and customers.

The theory of complex systems thinking does not only apply to small private sector companies, but also to large multi-national companies and yes, wait for it ... the public sector. I have been working with one Local Authority for over a year, changing the managers to leaders and removing the notion of traditional 'management' from that organisation.

I have maintained, for several years now, that all the simple things have been done to death, in most Business  Schools, in business theory and in consultancy, and that now only the 'messy' things are left. But it's the messy things that matter. It's the messy things that make the difference to sustainable leadership and innovation in Services. What I want is thinking around a simple architecture for seeing and understanding how natural, human systems, such as people and organisations, operate while recognising system uncertainty. It helps 'leaders' understand that the behaviour of people within the organisation and their interactions influence the design and direction of the whole organisation.

How many times have we seen seemingly sound strategies fail at the implementation stage? How many more times do we have to experience the alterations and failure of plans in a new hospital build or sports centre buildings before we are able to understand and accept that it is messy, simply because people are messy? Most things we do in any industry or service involve people. It's about time we understood the rules of the 'people game'.

I feel strongly that organisations are human, not 'systems' where the parts can be replaced like cogs in a machine. This is an adaptive system which cannot be controlled by the traditional managerial mind-set. Indeed, the more measures, procedures and rules that are created by managers the less effective the organisation becomes – the very opposite to what is commonly believed.

We only have to look at 'efficiency' target setting by the NHS or the police force to realise that whilst targets have been met, doctors' morale is still at an all time low and absenteeism amongst police officers is at an all time high. Managerial meddling is bringing industry and public services to their knees by a desire to control, plan and limit the interaction of staff.

It's always anathema to me that we champion democracy in all areas of our life except the workplace. This needs to change. I firmly believe that managers get in the way of staff who, if left to their own devices, would have the capability to satisfy customers. All these staff would need is to be supported by means of a system of trust, freedom and empowerment – and that is true empowerment, not delegation with small bells on it. At present managers simply get in the way of this organic process in most organisations, and that includes the public services as well as the manufacturing industry.

All managers should empower staff and sports professionals to make things happen – particularly to 'delight' the customer within the boundaries of budgets. Staff and front line workers should be trusted – as adults. We live in a democratic society outside of work, why should we have to be answerable to those above us in the workplace, who are not democratically elected? Why can't we be trusted to make the right decisions in line with the organisation's agreed values?

 Innovation, creativity, passion and adaptability are key to services and industry becoming sustainable entities and economic contributors with a true appreciation of the talent within.

# Chapter 2
## It Was a Strange Start to Management

*A man flying in a hot air balloon realised he was lost. Reducing altitude, he spotted a man on the ground and descended to shouting range.*

*"Excuse me," he shouted. "Can you help me? I promised my friend I would meet him a half hour ago, but I don't know where I am."*

*The man below responded: "Yes. You are in a hot air balloon, hovering approximately thirty feet above this field. You are between forty and forty-two degrees North Latitude, and between fifty-eight and sixty degrees West Longitude."*

*"You must be an engineer," responded the balloonist.*

*"I am," the man replied. "How did you know?"*

*"Well," said the balloonist, "Everything you have told me is technically correct, but I have no idea what to make of your information, and the fact is I am still lost."*

*Whereupon the man on the ground responded, "You must be a manager."*

*"That I am," replied the balloonist, "But how did you know?"*

*"Well," said the man, "You don't know where you are, or where you're going. You have made a promise which you have no idea how to keep, and you expect me to solve your problem. The fact is you are in the exact same position you were before we met, but now it is somehow my fault."*

In 1995, when I began teaching BSc students at a higher education college in England, it became almost a game for me to attempt to interest the students each term in the idea that sport, leadership and organisations were far more interesting than, to be honest, was actually the case.

Case studies on Google, BP, Shell, Rank Xerox ... I can almost feel the shudder going up the spines of my former students as I remember those days! This was all pretty sterile stuff compared to what I had experienced in management. They were of course historic, so we pretty much knew the outcomes, but even these were linear, rational, and reduced to simple meanings, added to which I mostly had the answers supplied along with the cases! I'm sure I have just shattered the sensitivities of most of my students who thought I actually understood and was knowledgeable in those unconnected 'cases' of business. Sorry about that! Indeed, between moments of strategic analysis, PEST Force analysis and SWOT analysis, I would regale my first week students in management with tales from my own history to break up the intense boredom (for me, not the students I might add!).

This would always start with the story of my first Saturday working as an Assistant Manager, at Aberfan Community Centre in South Wales.

Many will remember the Aberfan disaster in 1966. At that time coal tips surrounded most homes in the Welsh mining towns of the Valleys and on that terrible day in October 1966 one of these tips collapsed and engulfed a school and part of the street next to it. It had been a disaster waiting to happen as coal waste of mountainous proportions had been piled up over the bed of a stream. On the 21st of October it was raining heavily and the coal tip began to move.

A torrent of 'coal mud' was set free and moved at such a speed that it crushed everything in its path, and in that path was Pant Glas, Aberfan Primary School.  One hundred and sixteen children aged between 7 – 10 years of age, and twenty-eight teachers were killed – it was dark day in Welsh history.

My story, however, was about the day I walked into the memorial sports centre, built some fifteen years after the disaster. The Centre's Bar, run by the manager, Brian Lock, was full of people on this sunny Saturday afternoon.  With my clipboard tucked under my short-sleeved shirt and matching tie (a sort of uniform that I thought all managers were obliged to wear at that time, including the clipboard!), I looked in on Brian. Not to help, you understand – I had never run a bar in my life – but I was keen to show I was giving up my weekend to 'be there for him' if he needed help from a twenty-four year old, teetotal-non-drinking Assistant Manager with no experience at all!

I glanced through the door and noticed a horse at the bar, drinking from an ashtray (This is the point where I give my age away as I have to explain what an ashtray is, to my students!). I went up to my office at the top of the building and phoned down to Brian to ask him to come up and see me when he had two minutes to spare.

Brian was actually the perfect employee.  He was extremely hard working, dedicated and fast. Nothing was too difficult or presented an insurmountable challenge to Brian. Within seconds, almost before I managed to put the phone back on the hook, he had run up two flights of stairs, opened the door and sat down in the lower seats placed in front of my desk.

When I asked him, incredulously, if I had really seen a horse in the bar, because at this stage I doubted my own eyes, he shrugged and said, "Yes, that's right, and I am sorry but I don't see what the problem is. He (the horse) is a great drinker ... two pints at least, and his owner is a four pint man!" Brian saw everyone in terms of 'bar profits.' "Anyway," Brian continued, "he can't leave the horse outside, or some bugger will pinch it."

Nowhere in my management books had anyone prepared me for this kind of an eventuality in my first week. So I did the only thing I could think of and phoned my mother! I asked her opinion as to what I should do next. The outcome was that the horse continued to be made welcome, profits remained healthy, and Brian continued to impress and achieve results that I've never seen since!

I moved on to be an Assistant Manager at Merthyr Local Council. During my time there I experienced several cases of divorces, pregnancies and personal issues that the staff came to see me about. These were issues that, as a youngster, I was woefully unqualified to advise on. However, no doubt dazzled by my title of 'Mr Thomas – Assistant Manager', the staff were obviously convinced that I was eminently qualified to tackle even the weightiest personal problem.

My mother came into her own as I made many confidential calls home. One particular call gave her quite a shock when I began with, "Mam, I have a girl here who is pregnant and not sure if she wants to keep it or not." There was a long silence, which is very unusual for my mother, so as the penny dropped I said quickly, "Oh! No not me, I mean it's not my baby, no ... I mean I have a member of staff..." The relief on the other end of the phone was almost palpable and then came the incredulous question, "What on *earth* is she asking you for ...?"

## *Anyway, back to the book ...*

I had developed an early belief in positivism; that all things are real when expressed through numbers, structure and method, and that empirical truth can be established through experimentation and reproduction. All without subjective needs and processes of thought! I now find this difficult to accept. I find that even the most objective renderings of the real world do not provide an unbiased truth, detached from a subjective human viewpoint.

An example that I use in my lectures was first shown to me when I was lecturing in China in 2000. It is the now famous photograph of a Chinese student stopping a tank in Tiananmen Square, Beijing, 1989. This photograph shows the student standing in front of a large, powerful military vehicle representing an oppressive, mighty military force. This one image has provided the world with the knowledge that even a lone individual can make a difference to the path of history.

In China, however, this image is conveyed from a very different perspective – the *tank driver* is the hero, a man of great patience and skill who was able to avoid running over a troublesome and subversive individual. I believe, and have positioned this work from the viewpoint, that the perceived or received meanings of the viewer take precedence over the intended meaning of the producer.[1]

---

[1] subjective creation of meaning, explained further by Sarup, 1991 and Bourdieu 2005

Any text or story creates meaning the moment that it is seen by the viewer. From there it might be interpreted in a way that may not be what the original author had intended. Meanings are not therefore inherent in the text or image, but rather are the product of a complex social interaction between the text, the author, the reader and the cultural context. I would agree that dominant meanings emerge out of this complex social interaction, but this does not detract from my belief, or the position of this research, that individual interpretation is still a significant factor.

I now understand cultural meaning to be a highly fluid and changeable process that is the result of complex interaction among co-evolving individuals emerging because of the complex social processes of interpretation, engagement and negotiation (see Byrne 1999 for further detail). The 'manager', therefore, can be considered to be a fluid, changeable, complex and emerging individual who will, through interaction and the use of power, facilitate understanding about his or her position as a man or woman, a leader and an employee.

This premise presents the first theoretical position of my work and, I suppose, also presents the first problem. I simply struggle with the concept that 'tools' or models work in human organisations. They may do, to a point, but mostly people fail to understand fully the complete model and they experience slippage. In effect, they create their own meaning from words and stages and they will always take shortcuts, depending on who they are, in order to get to the goal; their goal – not the goal of the system or tool. Such is the reality of working with human beings!

**Teaching Business Managers. Warning, this gets a bit heavy going …**

*'It is necessary to recall an absolutely founding presumption of materialism: that the natural world exists whether anyone signifies it or not.'* (Williams, 1997: 167)

In 1999, I read a book by Ilya Prigogine in which this winner of the Nobel Prize for chemistry states that humankind is at a turning point because rational scientific research, which is identified with certitude and probability, has also brought with it – ignorance.

He remarks, insightfully, that we are currently witnessing, in management science, the birth of a new science that is no longer limited to idealised and simplified solutions, but reflects the complexities of individual agents (people) who inhabit the real world. His book helped focus my understanding of the human aspects of business and management, which led me to the anti-positivist attitude of Heidegger (described in Barnes, 1989) and to Searle (1993), in which there are no facts, only interpretations. The deconstruction of the 'actual' has challenged the western traditions of business academics and business writing, which until recently had regarded truth, objectivity and reality, as separate and measurable entities.

I found this discovery and, in the light of this knowledge, my subsequent work with various companies around the world, liberating. This was in part because I had previously been misled into thinking that science could be understood in isolation from the social, cultural, and political context in which it had developed. It was even more misleading to think of science as a timeline in which I memorised historical facts as a linear sequence of specific events. It was only when I was shown the film 'Memento' with Guy Pearce, that I really understood how difficult life is when we regard it as linear, factual, structured. And that's without looking at the failures in human perception.

Saunders, an American academic, provides an image that typifies the development of the history of science as a collection of campfires. She depicts *'campfires of thought'* (1998: 22) dotted around the social, cultural and political fields of their time. Each campfire represents the conceptual lessons of those gathered around it. She suggests that while all viewers can see and appreciate the flames that burn so brightly, they cannot hear the voices of those sitting around the fires, and instead concentrate on their own linear, mechanistic thoughts and the assumptions that take place around their own particular fire. This position and way of thinking are highlighted in most MBA programmes run in the UK, the USA and Australia probably to this day, with separate modules that the student will attempt in isolation of the bigger picture.

In 2001, after having attended a course at the London School of Economics, I began to change my area of interest from 'strategic management' to 'strategy in practice'.

This move was informed by a belief that began with my reading of Prigogine (1999) that suggested that in management studies we are dealing with complex evolving, fluid, dynamic systems – humans! These complex systems share the characteristics of nature's active participation in the world through interconnectedness, co-evolution, connectivity, and self-organisation (Middleton-Kelly 2004/5). This led me away from the image of the organisation as a machine and towards the more powerful tool of understanding typified by post-structuralism of individual agents and an organic system. Heraclites is credited with saying that it is impossible to step into the same river twice. He believed that the universe was characterised by constant change and that order results from the tension between two opposing forces. Whilst philosophical, it gives greater meaning to life, and indeed science's understanding of the world in which order means stagnation, stagnation means death, or ultimately being overwhelmed and subjugated by another more successful species. The Dodo and its inability to adapt to environmental competition is a good example of this. A creature that cannot adapt will eventually become extinct.

This idea of disorder, constant change, and the individual event, has some relevance in our world, as we can see and witness from a research and leadership perspective. In other words, nothing can be replicated; everything is unique and subject to change in the constantly flowing river of life.

This concept has allowed me to understand the dynamics of the real world in which managers make decisions. Not only are we anticipating and responding to change, which we realise we cannot control, but we are given another option: the ability to influence change as it emerges from organisations and not to rely blindly for our calculations on past trends to predict future events. You only have to look at the military to find an entity littered with examples of how planning in battle often fails catastrophically.

I have concluded, therefore, that the results of quantitative (numbers, stats, percentages) research in my field are generally unconvincing and represent the least useful way of attempting to understand the social world.

Yes, of course, this type of research can provide us with interesting patterns and trends that can, for example, highlight how many people experience bullying in the work place, but it's the qualitative stuff, the one-to-one interviews, that will ultimately and unfailingly yield the most interesting facts. Any 'numbers' based research will provide limited valuable scientifically significant results, but, in general, will not help to solve or explain the real issues that surround leadership and people.[2]

This is highlighted by the continued importance placed on the use of statistics in the business academy, and the increasing handicap of a lack of statistical skills for an academic who needs to publish work in this field. Byrne (1998: 87) comments that he is always 'annoyed by superficial and ignorant dismissal of the quantitative possibilities of

---

[2] Statistics and quantitative research does however provide valuable information with regards to patterns and trends. It is not my purpose to dismiss this approach, but rather highlight the reason for not adopting it in my research.

sociology', but it is still difficult for me to understand why statistical techniques, which have been developed in order to handle numbers, are still used to understand the real world of business and management. They reduce things such as motivation to single questions, and then in the narrow context of the organisation itself. But there is also considerable scope for bias using this method of analysis despite the use of numbers and statistical techniques that pretend to be objective, and that represent the Holy Grail for quantitative researchers. Those who scientifically design, test, and ask the questions introduce bias. They are only human after all, and wherever humans have a hand in anything an unavoidable bias, no matter how trivial or inconsequential, is inevitable. I accept that there will always be some degree of bias, I accept it in my research and welcome the fact that it is there – as an explanation of findings in a particular item of research. It allows me the opportunity to see the research with the bias and interest and, more importantly, allows my eyes to accept my own cultural and thinking bias.

From the outset, the position of this research has been simple. Education, leadership, and failures in traditional 'management' and its structures have all generated significant issues for me as a business academic and former manager. I now see that business schools have 'fitness landscapes', which are part of the reality of the social, political and global economic systems that surround business education.

To believe that there can be wholesale educational solutions for business and management is naïve, despite the present 'proliferation' of MBA's and business schools of which I am a part, within the global market. To state, as most business schools do, that managers should be able to understand their organisations, control their inputs and outputs, punish and reward their staff, and understand fully their operation, regardless of cultural location, is now not a realistic premise in my opinion. It is cruel to those attempting this pursuit and harmful to those trying to implement it, as well as being injurious to those on the receiving end of such impossible ideals.

Mintzberg (2004) stated that managers must develop the notion that they are dealing, within their workforce, with individuals – each with their own perspectives, vision, and needs. Stacey (2004) supports this and comments that managers should become 'gardeners', and tend to their gardens (organisations) in a natural, organic and influential way rather than in a controlled way. This was, and still is, an important position for work in the field over the past ten years, for whilst I don't fully buy into the Ralf Stacey world of human systems, I do like the natural metaphor and garden description when used in relation to leadership and companies. Why? Because I feel that as an educator in leadership, developing the 'thinking skills' of the managers, it is important to understand the 'habitus' of the individual.

When you see leaders in action you gain a far greater insight than is possible from any model or theory. I often come across 'leaders' who, while they are not in formal positions and do not fit into any model of popular leadership, are nevertheless leading brilliantly!

# Chapter 3
## So what is a manager? More theory ...!

One way to understand my research is in relation to contemporary management discourses. If Drucker (1993) represents the dominant influence in management science and taught management studies, then Argyris (1978), Senge (1991), Stacey (2003), Mintzberg (2001, 2002, 2004) and Kelly (2004) represent a move away from this influence to a more humanistic, agency-based model.

The development towards human-centred management theory reflects the need for a new basis for the discipline, in the light of a growing distrust in past scientific theory and fear over future practice (Mintzberg, 2004). My research on managers and this thing we call 'leadership' follows the humanist model in appreciating the importance of the individual and the impact that individuals have on organisations.

This is not to negate the importance of scientific rigour, validity, or reliability, but simply to state my position as a poststructuralist, as I have explained previously. Post structuralism for me is a set of theoretical positions that require practitioners to participate in a self-reflective discourse with perpetual awareness of the tentativeness, slipperiness, ambiguity and complexity that exists in relation to text and meanings (Sarup, 1993).

Consequently, my work emphasises the importance of subjective and individual changes that provide a framework to make sense of the everyday situated experiences of my subjects. My intention and belief is, therefore, that I will never discover the reality of the managers I work with in any company, but that I can help to construct a reality. I cannot remove myself from the research process (May 2001). The truth here is constructed from my interactions as a teacher, researcher, pro-feminist and complexity thinker.

The social relationships of these managers within a company and outside are always incomplete (Bourdieu 2005). In real terms this means that I never really see the true person I am dealing with in any situation in life, I only see what they want me to see, and only after time, in a business context, do I get to appreciate truly their leadership skills or lack of them.

This is often experienced in communities that do not recognise their leadership as discrete (or viable), filtered through competing discourses of identity. I will argue that without adopting the poststructuralist perspective, it is not possible to understand the specifics of the manager's role, its impact on others and its existence, since there are no finite social practices inherent in its identity, only what we as individuals place onto this concept of 'manager' from education, but more so past experience.

In the changing economic climate of the world and regions, the role of manager is seen as both fluid and dynamic, as political and personal issues respond to market economics, seemingly free from the status quo that would have determined our experience in the same arena fifty years ago.

My book and work reflects my innate dissatisfaction with the management 'beast', the constant tinkering with the broken engine, and the downright harmful 'consultancy' culture that seems to offer 'quick' solutions to issues, but that in truth only delays the resolution of major problems, creating a long term role for the consultancy organisation.

I will also moan about failed initiatives such examples as the drive towards I.T. as the solver of all problems. The NHS failures to implement an I.T. system that cost billions is an excellent if tragic example. I.T .wizards/geeks will no doubt be shouting, 'I know I.T. is not a solution!'

My argument is with the sacred cow of I.T. wheeled in by managers, consultants or, worse still, politicians to increase efficiencies as a common example of reductionist thinking.....simple problem, simple solution failing. It is the fact that they do not look first to the front line – because that supposes they (the front line) are doing their job – that gives me my major gripe. My work simply highlights workers' lived experiences, the changes possible, and, of course, also presents some 'what you do next' advice.

I believe, that leadership experience needs to be more fully theorised and explored, not from the traditional 'what makes a good leader?' point of view but by asking the question – where is leadership within the organisation?

I also contend that the failure to develop models of experience as partial, fragmented and contradictory, limits our ability to make sense of, and thus fully understand, the reality of organisations, their successes, failures and their resilience in the 21st Century.

I also accept that any work by academics in the field of business carries and provokes a certain suspicion, both from other academics and 'real people.' I accept this wariness, but that will not stop me challenging the concept of management and for that matter leadership. As a 'failed manager' and practising academic, and having worked in over twenty-eight companies, I still feel guilty for any unintentional oppression of 'free thinkers' and people who do great things on instinct.

I have gained enormous insight, liberation, and a sense of purpose by leaving the ranks of the 'oppressors', and in academia resisting merely teaching by rote from a textbook or core themes. I will no longer be part of the domination and subordination of half of the human race simply because I was born male, western or hold a 'qualification'. In management academe there are a few great scholars who teach from the hip, providing reality to youngsters and returning professionals, and I hope I am still hanging in there with a shout!

The battle has been really tough. I was warned once by an academic in the LSE that 'doing' complexity and being within a traditional business school would be 'agony', and I had to be prepared for grief if I was going to try and change the system, and to be disliked and treated with suspicion. He wasn't wrong.

The journey has been incredibly arduous. I was introduced, at the beginning of my 'tenure' at Glamorgan University, now called the University of South Wales, to a group of doctorate students as Doctor Bollocks! Why? Well, put simply, the professor, who had grown to know his students over time, obviously felt relaxed in front of them. He had to introduce me and what I was about to talk about, which was 'Complexity in leadership and a post structural stance'. This was a subject that he knew very little about, had chosen to ignore, or simply disagreed with. That being the case he simply could not be bothered to put on a front. He said, "I'd like now to introduce Paul, whose research into the field of ... what is it? ... .oh yes, Complexity and Postie stuff, which I have to say seems all bollocks to me [*class laughs nervously*], here is ... well... Doctor of Bollocks ... Paul."

I have to say that I did feel quite stunned, but I managed a reply; "Well, thank you for that Professor ... I have received some truly excellent, thought provoking, and intelligent introductions in my time as guest speaker... but that wasn't one of them!" and I carried on regardless.

I was known on campus for about two years after that as Dr Bollocks. And I suppose you will have realised by now that from this incident came the title of this book, as the 'battles' with managers, management and daft professors seemed to take a hold of my life. However, I look back at my time in Glamorgan with fondness. After all, the issues there led me to

where I am now, and have allowed me to achieve this great success, so I suppose I should thank that dinosaur of a professor.

I have to mention someone else who came later on in Glamorgan, a wonderful Dean, Professor Alan Lovell (opps). He is retired now and enjoying life away from the political battles of Glamorgan University, which I am sure wore him down at an incredible rate. I mention him as he was one of the very few people who 'got it' and saw the potential in this work, and allowed me great freedom and trust. He was one of the rare 'leaders' I talk about in this work who stood for the people and drove outputs not from micro-managed rules, but from real values. You simply didn't want to let him down.

This didn't last, as with all organisations great people like Professor Alan retire or move on and any small gains they have managed are lost. In this case the new Dean was brought in to cost-cut and remove anyone who could argue back, and generally to suppress 'curiosity'. It is true to say that I have not benefited professionally from my anti-management non-traditional stance. Quite the opposite has been my experience, as under the new regime, and to underline the deep suspicion that surrounded what I did, I was soon 'let go' with the Dean stating openly, "I don't know what he does." So I left, taking with me substantial research and business funds, lots of work and a BBC Documentary Series, which was taking the viewers by storm.

This new Dean by the way, did what was supposed to look like the decent thing and promoted me into a job that didn't exist, then declared one month after the reorganisation that the role no longer existed. I tell this story not to let you think that I in any way regret what happened at that time. I don't. In fact, I would hasten to say that I would not change a thing in my journey, other than the hardship, trouble and worry I've brought on my family over the years, wondering what on earth was coming next. Apart from that, it's been great fun!

Anyhow…..There is also the context of organisation itself. March and Simon (1993:2) write that an organisation is a *'system of coordinated actions among individuals and groups whose preferences, information, interests and knowledge differ'.* If this is so, then the central task of an organisational manager is *'the delicate conversion of conflict into cooperation'* (p.2). Such conversions are greatly assisted when the participants speak a common language and share access to somewhat similar views of the world they inhabit. Cultural values associated with workers, and then managers, are characteristics favoured by many organisations to support a 'common view', or what some would deem culture. Management is often mirrored in organisational practice that emphasises rationality, control, certainty and bureaucracy, while suppressing the sentiments normally associated with leadership, such as emotion, feeling, passion and warmth.

I first experienced the practice of a 'worker' organisation as a young adult in my first job as a lifeguard. Everything in the lifeguard team centred on male cultural issues, even to the point that female lifeguards were discouraged for being 'weak' and 'unable to rescue anyone bigger than a child'. In three years whilst I was at college, and 'on the pool' at several different organisations, I only ever worked with one female lifeguard, and that was for a very short period of time. For the rest of the time my colleagues and fellow male lifeguards were very typical sportsmen, such as Peter, his brother 'Ginger' (aka Martyn), and Glyn.

The assumptions based on sex and gender as described above manifest themselves in a number of ideas and practices determined by social identities and experiences. Mills (2002) noted that certain organisations play a direct part in the socialising processes in which people acquire gender identity such as schools, sports teams and state departments that more often than not conform to, and extend, sex-based values. Like

49

Mills (1992), I argue that sexual discrimination is not only seen in overt organisational practices but especially in sports management itself, which is saturated with cultural values that then permeate both the organisations and the concept of the organisation itself.

This early personal experience of the management and career progress of women initially prompted me to explore how sports and recreation had impacted on their lives, in order to understand the effects of their perceived boundaries of management from a sports and cultural position. I had hoped, perhaps, that my involvement with the lives of Chinese women managers through my MBA teaching would subsequently provide further insights into the ways that cultural identities are perceived and structures developed – a better understanding of the way that the fabric of managerial life affected the image and participation of women working in management.

My personal sporting activity added an important dimension to my experience and subjectivity as a male with a sense of maleness (Whitson, 1994).

Scratton's (1992) work on education and girls' culture points to the material constraints of finance, opportunities and access, and the ideological constraints of domesticity and sub-cultural values. These factors, together with the socio-economic, ethnic, and geographic backgrounds of individuals, all provide varying barriers to women's participation, or so I found, in my earlier experiences of sport.

Through sport and my own sense of my masculinity in my early career, it began to dawn on me that my masculinity was fluid and situational, and that there was no hard and fast category. I was male on the rugby field and feminine in the house. I don't mean I wore dresses or called myself Paula, but at home I would show more feminine traits, be involved in more traditionally feminine activities, as described in gender studies. So, if there were a mixture of gender bias in all individuals in normal life perhaps, I thought, leadership in organisations could be fluid, situational and contextual as well.

# Chapter 4
# Let's do the opposite to beat the rot!

Panic, fear and mistrust are everywhere in business. At the time of writing this book another global economic recession is hitting the UK (and most parts of the world) and the inevitable job cutting and financial hardships have returned with a vengeance. This will bring about an even greater mistrust which is spreading, not just in business but also to banking, the public sector and even to our National Health Service.

"Oil prices and commodity prices increase as a result of a need to maintain control and profits as demand outstrips supply. People will lose jobs as the pace of business slows, leading to a rise in the national unemployment rate. Housing prices will continue to decline. Building and construction companies will grind to a halt and people will eventually stop spending, frightened into saving instead. The stock market decline will continue until the market sees evidence of the beginning of a new period of business expansion, confidence and when trust is restored."

This is an extract from an article I wrote in 2008. The truth is that recessions are unavoidable and are a normal part of the cycle of economics, or human systems. That being so, I could save this article and republish it every ten years or so and still be very current! So, if this is a recurring and natural event, dealing with it should be fairly straightforward, and the big players in terms of countries will have a contingency plan for this very situation. Yes? Well actually – no.  So no surprise there then.  The manufacturing base has been trying to change their approach for years and prepare for such events without much luck it seems. There are exceptions such as SEMCO in Brazil who work on the notion of speed and adaptability. We have known for some time that companies who try to compete on cost and low price will suffer the most. To survive, each company, service and product must have a value-added element, and not merely offer cheap alternatives, which tends to be the norm.

In all companies we must look to diversify our markets, seek niche rather than mass markets, and strive to individualise products. This is where the company that invests in its employees, removes the tribal 'managers v employees' culture and opts instead for empowered, democratic working practices, will triumph.

This is achieved by trusting in staff to help sort out further reductions and efficiencies, removing tiers of managers to add more value to frontline production, innovation and diversity, and *truly* empowering staff. That will be the only way to operate in the next few decades.

In short, to survive the global recession or any other assault on productivity and successful endeavour, whether local or global, we need to control fear, trust staff, be financially prudent, create innovative products and services, and look to empower staff, not managers. This is what will help us through the tough times ahead. It's simple, so you can stop reading now ... I've peaked!

Okay, maybe a little premature! The role model of a chief executive in tomorrow's world will be one who is prepared to break all the traditional rules and succeed through people – by democratic principles of engaging everyone in the organisation to lead. One constant quote I hear from great Leaders is 'My only task is to ensure people are allowed to be great leaders. To make sure the environment is right to grow talent"....simple yet true.

The key is that all CEO's should get paid less than frontline staff, be voted into office by frontline staff, only receive a bonus if they have been seen to listen, and help implement the frontline drive to create and satisfy custom, margins, quality and performance.  It seems that this is likely to be the only way the future will work – letting employees choose what they do, where and when they do it, and even how they get paid.  This concept is too upside-down for most managers, but this is the future, as I hope my work will prove.

Maybe the new way for the brave new world of business is about letting go of power and instead having the skill to influence people through core values rather than strategy and rules.

I often ask managers who are also parents, "Do you manage total control of your children?" They nearly always laugh and reply with an emphatic, "No!" Yet we think nothing of trying to exercise control over fully grown adult people in the workplace – we tell them what time to come in, what time to leave, we even give them a 'job description' for goodness sake, which we all know is a daft concept given that the first thing aggrieved unions threaten is a work to rule.

That leads to us observing that working in strict adherence to the job description (rule) brings the company to a virtual standstill! If we treat employees like children, they will react and act like children, and so the downward spiral goes as we react by putting in more rules, regulations, and measures, and if all this fails, another tier of supervision. By doing this, we are simply reinforcing the notion that the workforce are children. And even if we accepted the premise that the workforce is 'child-like', they are very unlikely to be as familiar as our own children. We rarely get to know most of the people in our companies very well, if at all, so how on earth do we expect to control them if we cannot even control our own children with whom we live?

The answer is that we don't, and we should not even try to, but what we must try to do is *influence*.

Influence is not control as it is emergent, and co-evolved. We must begin by attacking the 'corporate oppression' seen in the layer upon layer of managers with status, perceived control, and hierarchy. This can be achieved by removing time clocks, dress codes, security procedures, privileged office receptionists and secretaries. Why not let everyone meet their own visitors, send their own faxes, make their own coffee?

Buying talent, not time, will be the key to success for any future business leader. Indeed, the future leader will only attain that position after being elected by those they are about to lead, not by his or her own seniors. To reduce workload and get more people involved in taking decisions the layers of needless hierarchy must be eliminated.

The thought that frontline workers could directly influence their own pay and thus encourage leaders to look for savings, and to question any procedures or layers of management that didn't seem to add value, seems a distant hope. Adding value from the customer's perspective is the core function of any business yet this is often forgotten in the manager's pursuit for self-preservation, salary protection and a focus on moving up the corporate ladder.

Managers in the future will be hired and fired by frontline staff, and kept only as long as they 'add value'. Future managers will allow accounts and budget to be visible and influenced by all in the organisation. More than that, the units will invent new businesses for themselves.

Future managers will need to see themselves as the **'questioner'**, the **'challenger'** and the **'catalyst'** of all that is done and will be done in the organisation, and not perhaps in the traditional role of the creator of the new. They will be the person who asks basic questions and encourages people to bring things down to the simplest level; to apply common sense to complicated issues. They no longer need to be involved in day-to-day affairs and, in fact, this will be the last concern as the frontline deal with all operational issues.

The key skill is therefore 'workplace democracy'. Many are still sceptical that such a radical way of managing can actually work, but those who already do this see immediate benefits such as increased profits, more innovation and a workforce truly empowered and wanting to go to work each morning.

The other key for managers in the future is to create trust in the organisation and beyond. Where there is trust there is an increase in risk, and with that risk, supported by all, there will be an immediate increase in creativity and innovation.

Managers will need to give people the freedom to do what they want, and accept that over time their successes will far outweigh any failures. It seems that if you trust people to do the right thing, and if it's obviously in their interest to do so, then they will do their best to make it happen.

# My Top Tips for 21st Century Leaders

- Forget about the bottom line stuff – the top line is key in achieving the bottom-line. Think values, purpose, pride, passion and people.
- Create the passion that most businesses start with. If you've forgotten it, then re-establish with all the staff ... it's a great thing to do the 'why are we here?' questions.
- Don't always focus on growth – some companies are better small or niche – remember it's about fun, passion, adding value and making a living ...
- Never stop being a leader of people – you cannot switch leadership off. Even when you are not doing it people still gain energy, safety and comfort from your presence.
- Concentrate on attitude, not skills for the job/role – skills are important of course, especially if you are a surgeon, but attitude counts much more. Just ask a patient in your care.
- Treat people like adults and not children – if you treat people like most managers do, like five year olds, they will act like five year olds. The consequence is that you will spend most of your time wiping bottoms and chasing people around the room. Treat workers like adults and expect adult problems ... you will be a leader in no time.
- Buy talent and output, but never time. Don't focus on inputs such as sitting at the desk or asking permission to attend a seminar. Just focus on outputs, outputs and outputs – value-added to the customer driven outputs. Allow the frontline staff

to concentrate on the outputs, quality, performance and of course value. You'll be amazed and the levels they reach if you don't interfere.

- Make decisions quickly and openly, and gather partners, promiscuously. Don't ever think they won't be able to cope with the news/honesty. If you don't tell them, most in the company will make stuff up. And remember to guide your talks, decisions around the purpose of the organisation not the details.
- Listen, and truly understand the art of listening to others. It's a tough one, believe me. Most people pretend to listen. How can you tell? They utter 'ah-ums' or 'mmms', or simply look away from you as they search for additional things to tell you about themselves. That's not listening. Oh and once you have listened, act! Do something so show you have listened.
- Accept that companies will be employee and not management controlled – stick to leading the core boundaries and not the details.
- Don't seek permission to make decisions. The leader's role will only be to influence and check values are driven and it's the purpose at the core.
- Focus on results and not process. Simply ask, 'who's delighted by this work'? and then ask what are the margins and added values.
- Remember, employees are accountable, not managers.

Strategies are being written and human resource departments formed to issue policies and plan careers, while entrepreneurs are being pushed to the margins where they are less disruptive. It's wrong, and it's not necessary. If there are a hundred employees in the company then we need them all to be leaders/managers ... a hundred managers, not one.

| Conventional Manager | Future Leader (You) |
|---|---|
| Focus on process development | Focus on organisational development – think of it as a person! |
| Focus on hardware and equipment | Focus on humans – make it individuals-always |
| | Focus on the boundaries which are immovable |
| Focus on efficiency | Focus on job satisfaction, output, happiness and trust |
| Systems specified by technologists | User-specified systems Individualise – give allowance to buy their own hardware |
| Rule-oriented action Hierarchic, bureaucratic | Autonomy, creativity, values Democratic, organic, evolutionary |
| Adapted from McMillan 2010 | |

# Chapter 5
# The Pitfalls and Pain: A Director's view

*The British and the Japanese decided to engage in a competitive boat race. Both teams practised hard and long to reach their peak performance. On the big day they felt ready.*

*The Japanese won by a mile. Afterward, the British team was discouraged by the loss. Morale sagged. Corporate management decided that the reason for the crushing defeat had to be found, so a consulting firm was hired to investigate the problem and recommended corrective action.*

*The consultant's finding: the Japanese team had eight people rowing and one person steering; the British team had one person rowing and eight people steering.*

*After a year of study and millions spent analysing the problem, the consultant firm concluded that too many people were steering and not enough were rowing on the British team.*

*So as race day neared again the following year, the British team's management structure was completely reorganised. The new structure: four steering managers, three area steering managers and a new performance review system for the person rowing the boat to provide work incentive.*

*The next year, the Japanese won by two miles. Humiliated, the British corporation laid off the rower for poor performance and gave the managers a bonus for discovering the problem ...*

## *And back to the book ...*

The case study below records a twenty-four month period within an SME as the company embraced natural system thinking and explains how people changed from stressed out controlled 'machines' into a freethinking, self-organising team of highly motivated individuals. It records the problems of introducing Simplexity in a random manner and how these problems were overcome. The study suggests how leaders – thinking differently, releasing control and relinquishing power – can improve business systems, although it has to be appreciated that there will be an initial period of difficulty, unrest and conflict. It also suggests that, with a leadership belief that fosters trust and enables culture to grow from within, people will unlock their potential and contribute to the ever-changing landscape of their work environment. What follows diaries an experiment that began in late 2002 to evaluate the relationships between business and natural systems theory in order to develop a working environment which eliminates the causes of stress and unlocks human potential, innovation and evolution.

## Background

'WhichWay Solutions' began trading in 2000 and was formed to provide innovative recruitment, training, and staffing solutions to contact centres at various locations in the UK. The board of directors consisted of John Ward and another shareholder. They both had a background in sales and John also had experience of recruitment, education and training.

This was, at the time, an area where poor recruitment was severely hampering the successful growth of call centres, one of the UK's growing industries, resulting in high staff turnover, low morale, and increased staff sickness. From 2000-2005, WhichWay Solutions doubled its turnover and profits year on year, and staff numbers grew to fifty-two. As the company grew, traditional hierarchical structures were 'naturally' introduced by the directorship without any real intent or purpose.

## The problems

As the company grew and became more hierarchical, the co-director quietly took over the day-to-day 'management of people', making it his responsibility to ensure the efficient use of employee resources and to direct customer projects, and John stepped back into connecting and creating new business. It became clear, after two years, that the two directors had quite differing and contradicting leadership styles and thoughts about how the company should operate.

One key incident that occurred in 2002 brought things to a head. In the absence of John, the co-director segmented the business into three Individual Business Units (IBU's) so that they could operate more effectively and be managed by an increasing number of policies and procedures. These IBU's were Recruitment, Training and NVQ Assessing. Targets were set for activity and revenue and these were reviewed weekly in an open meeting. This traditional approach quickly led to a culture of separation between employees and management with all the associated problems. Everyone ignored these consequences initially. Company turnover was increasing so this approach remained consistent for the next three years. A further layer of management was introduced in 2002 with the appointment of a general manager and a training manager to co-ordinate the operations and deal with the ever increasing staff problems such as low morale, high turnover and sickness absence.

However, by the end of 2003, the imposed structure in the company had totally collapsed. Staff simply found the structure too restrictive and unhelpful in daily operations. The informal structure grew back and subverted the formal. The top-down pressure had, it seemed, also changed the dynamics of a previously close-knit team. They had become separate, un-communicative individuals, while their fear of ridicule in the highly control-orientated culture began to affect their health, causing stress and illness. As a result, two of the original IBU leaders resigned from the company, citing the fact that they had suffered with unnecessary pressure caused by the re-structure and co-director's style as the reason for their departure.

Throughout this difficult period the boardroom conflict continued to bubble under the surface. The issues, although clearly visible to staff, were not acknowledged by the directors who denied that any problem existed. This combined with the misguided notion that a managing director should act 'on the business', reinforced the breakdown in communication. One employee commented to me that John had become, "unapproachable, not too involved in the business, and really scary." (emp9). They also added that most staff felt he had stepped back because he wasn't interested or committed to the business any longer, with most citing a fear he was about to sell-up and leave the company. This was not the case.

Meanwhile, between 2004 and 2006, both directors studied for an MBA on which I was teaching. Classmates voiced the opinion that they thought we were fortunate to be able to apply different tools as various subjects were addressed. Still in the traditional mind-set, the directors did what every new MBA'er does and set about using every tool in the MBA tool bag taught on the course, with mixed reviews!

These top-down interventions and use of tools had not been thought through enough for their company and context, and were not working to improve relationships within the organisation. Instead they were breaking existing goodwill and relations. The staff complained of continual unsettling changes, changes for change sake, and feelings of insecurity and stress.

The directors, not aware of the feelings of staff, went on regardless – strategy planning, setting target after target, analysing internal and external forces and measuring all the wrong things, such as productivity, phone call efficiency and paper turnover. An example of all this was that they believed that targeting staff to visit learners twice a month would guarantee a high delivery quality. What they discovered was that the visiting staff were so focussed on recording the visits that achieved their targets that they forgot why they were visiting in the first place!

These are typical comments from that time:

*"Communication wasn't there because there was always that barrier. You couldn't go straight to the source, you had to go through the middle man; you couldn't go and deal with that person directly, it was as though you kind of didn't feel like you could be very honest or upfront about things [with X] because you knew you'd get it in the neck the next day."* (J, July 2006)

*"With X, if we would talk about something she'd say she would 'filter it down to John' and then when I would mention it to him, John hadn't been told. Someone would always be out of the loop. There was mis-communication or no communication at all when there was the three of you and it was frustrating."* (L, July 2006)

*"X only lets you hear what she wanted you to hear."* (B, July 2006)

The new imposed management structure confirmed the real conflict in the leadership styles on the board. Freedom and trust versus command & control; no control versus activity targets and the obsessive measuring of everything. Staff were given some freedom but if something went wrong, they were hastily reeled back in and controlled by the other director.

The company became passionate about issuing targets for everything, and then not measuring them very well. When they did measure them, they used negative feedback techniques to keep staff on-track, which further eroded the connectivity, trust and energy within the already disconnected team.

Despite all this the business continued to grow. John, in fairness, identified that the disjointed leadership styles were causing a huge amount of stress for the staff that remained, but this was only after a bare-all session, which I would never recommend under any circumstances as they can quickly become aggressive and highly damaging in both the short and the long term. There was a problem here with management power, their perceived status, communication and, of course, the changes brought about by the MBA 'world' that had led to or increased a breakdown in relationships.

# My DNA intervention

It is important to stress at this point that the directors or should I say John (he won't mind me saying this..) made a lot of mistakes before DNA intervened trying to use the Simplexity way. The description that follows is a brief summary of what I, in combination with the Directors, and John in particular, did, and how it affected the company. It is not a road map for others to follow but may help to explain the importance of having an open mind, allowing risk, understanding that you must understand the theory of Simplexity, not taking one of the elements and supporting efforts that fail, all in a positive manner. For me positive means energy, it does not mean smiling even when things go wrong, but making sure there is effort to move things out of failure, not just dwell on the problems/faults.

First of all John and the other director looked constantly for ways to improve communication and involve people in the process, which was brilliant. John is gregarious, charming, and an excellent communicator, but coming from a 'sales' world found that they had used what most managers use to involve staff – 'selling the idea' or more accurately the sinister sounding 'social engineering', which is more transparent and dangerous than most would like to admit.

In November 2004, both directors began the process by facilitating a DNA concept 'Moan & Groan' (M&G) session to help identify possible causes and possible consequences of under-performance in certain key areas. This M&G session is simply where members of staff are able, without managers, to say what they think, from what's wrong to what's right. They also get a chance to state what they would change immediately if they were in charge, and had an endless supply of money. The session, which we now call 'Stage 1' (more of this at the end of the book) worked like this: At the start, all managers are removed and then the questions begin; What's wrong? – Who is at fault? – What can we change first thing in the morning? – What can be changed by the end of the week? – What are the tougher areas we must change? – What makes you happier in work? – What are the key things that make your job harder? ... and so on!

From this process, the team itself proposed a new structure in which 'experts' would be used to deliver key services whilst the remainder had time to learn from them. Controls were to be released and activity targets dropped. It's worth pointing out that this type of 'Moan & Groan' (M&G) session is vital if an organisation is to move forward. A warning though......these sessions can get quite heated. At one meeting, the moans and groans were so extensive that I had to bring in my former colleagues, Dr Kelly Page and John Batten, to help record all the issues.

I always remember working with a Local Authority where the highways men and gullies men were looking to fight one another over the problem of overtime. The bone of contention was that the gullies men would get overtime in the rain, and times of flood risk. The highways men, who once had abundant funds to fill tarmac holes in over weekends, found themselves without even the basic funds to do even the most simplest? job in the week times. This left a lot of unspoken tension, which I unknowingly to me released in an M&G session. Needless to say I spent the time physically holding apart some quite angry men wanting to hit lumps out of each other.

Another session, after we had collected all the moans, groans and what next tips, turned nasty because I had forgotten to reinforce the issue that they would be starting the 'to-do-list' first thing next morning. The staff at one company, which employed around fifty workers, simply refused to do anything that would help the company, as it *was the managers' fault* (this is my worry about most traditional companies that have a 'them and us' culture), and it was the managers who should put it right.

This, however, is a much tougher, slower and more frustrating proposal, and managers normally need to be convinced through statistics, evidence and facts, which under this immediate process are never available. This means then I have to provide an academic argument to a mind-set and group who don't really see there is a problem in the first place. If they did they would not be in the position they are in or would simply opt to attend one of my classes to do it themselves.

Sessions can also take some strange turns. At one session recorded by BBC Radio Wales, microphones were placed on the tables of a factory canteen. I was concerned that the workers would not really be able to express themselves with their every comment, moan and groan recorded for the Welsh nation. However, I could not have been more wrong! Half-way through the session one of the workers, a young girl sitting on a fixed four seat table of the type found in most canteens, shouted, "*Cor, you could be the father of my baby any day.*

71

*You're alright you are*"... I laughed and carried on asking for 'issues.' "Anything we could change tomorrow with a magic wand?" Yes, you've guessed it. As soon as the word 'wand' left my lips all the women burst into laughter and the girl who had asked me to father her baby piped up again, "*I wouldn't mind seeing your wand. I reckon it could work magic on me alright, especially if I got my wishes.*"

I have to confess that by this time I was bright red, not as a result of being the target of this young woman's affection, but because in the raucous banter that followed it was revealed that the girl was already pregnant, apparently by one of the lads in production. And the Jeremy Kylesque scene did not stop there as the lad concerned fervently denied any wrong doing with the girl. The room fell about with laughter and there followed a lively and heated discussion over the identity of the child's father! The final conclusion was that the girl had been so drunk one night over Christmas that the baby's father could be the brother of the accused, and possibly one of many others! Despite the constant, "*Guys ... remember this is being recorded live for radio*" plea, in the vein hope this would stop such revelations, any hope of propriety had to be abandoned. So much for a public forum inhibiting expression!

Although the team were beginning to understand the benefits of the new structure, there were still problems. There was freedom, but no-one was taking responsibility. The general manager was using a degree of control that went against our intentions.

Anyhow, back to the case. It was at this point they decided to enlist my help formally as the business doctor, as I had started to open their eyes to the possibilities of embracing Simplexity as a way of improving the business. I always start with a non-academic introduction to Complex Evolving Systems when I speak to a workforce, in an attempt to explain the new way of thinking the company will adopt.

The effect this had was the opposite of what I hoped. Within three hours, the workforce's belief system had been destroyed, and the command and control background that they had previously known and felt safe in was gone for ever. Almost everyone in the team saw this 'different way of thinking' as a threat and as something that wouldn't work. Very few saw it as a positive move. This confirms that, unlike the way cause and effect freaks think, the effect, far from having an equal or uniform impact, will vary with the state of each related individual and system experienced. This is a theme that repeats itself at every point of disturbance and far-from-equilibrium state that we find ourselves in.

This uncertainty and discomfort that people felt was to stay with them for the next nine months until we could prove the validity of our approach. When asked how he would describe the company in July 2006, a staff member stated: *"To have the opportunity to think differently. Like a liberating experience because all the controls and barriers you're used to have gone, you're free to have ideas, change things, shift directions. There are no limits to what we can do."*

By May 2005, the new structure that the team had introduced in November 2004 had further evolved – through peer pressure, mostly. *"It just grew out of itself,"* one internal staff member commented (R, July 2006). This new structure had temporarily enabled the company to improve on the key skills performance, and had also proved to those who were apprehensive about taking on the responsibility, that it was possible to learn new skills. This realisation meant that most

NVQ assessors retained the right to deliver key skills, and in turn this would eventually make the job of 'skills specialists' redundant.

Some were still struggling with the responsibility and control this change brought, so it was decided to perturb the system with the radical change of removing the management structure altogether, an idea enthusiastically bought by John Ward. At a team meeting in May 2005, it was announced that the management structure would be removed. This was met by the following suggestion from an assessor: *"As the general manager would no longer be dealing with Performance Development Reviews, why couldn't team members be anonymously evaluated by other team members themselves?"*

At this point, they were frustrated with the slow pace of change. The Directors made the mistake of intervening and suggested dividing the existing team structure into two teams. This decision was partly based on the successful work of Ricardo Semler who operates his companies in teams of eight to twelve people. As they had now grown to twenty-one staff and recruited another MBA graduate, they assumed that this would improve communication.

It was during May that 'management' was removed. People were in turmoil over this radical way of thinking and it became apparent to me that there was still conflict between the leadership styles of John and his traditional co-director. One employee was very perceptive in an observation he made of the situation: *"You could see differences of opinions and differences in how things would happen. You tended to let things happen but he was more reserved and more scared of what would happen if he let go."* (R, 2006)

Although John's co-director had claimed to be committed to the Simplexity view of operation in the company, it was obvious that he didn't truly believe in it as practice. I discovered, via a conversation with John, that he was exploring all of the reasons Simplexity would not work in our company as part of his dissertation at MBA level. At any hint of uncertainty in practice, he would always revert to command and control methods of target setting and measuring activities, which instantly undermined the push to more democratic and human thinking. It was for this reason that John removed his power and assumed the position of facilitator to help embed Simplexity into WhichWay Ltd.

John also realised that he was taking a back seat and as Lewin (2003) maintains, 'someone has to facilitate the generation of knowledge without attempting to control it'. He goes on to say, 'they need to create an environment in which creativity can emerge in bounded stability'. This meant agreeing boundaries. It was obvious that the team were feeling vulnerable without traditional structure and no boundaries had been created or discussed so a workshop with me was convened to discuss team boundaries and explain a little more about the desired organisation.

This was not successfully completed however, which led to increased frustration from some, as stated by one here: *"We were talking about 'boundaries', but we didn't actually finish talking about that, so at the moment the boundaries have only half been set if you like. There are definitely mixed messages there."* (B, Secondary research October 2005)

R disagrees with this view and says: *"Change is not a conscious decision but more a group decision. It's not even talked about but still it stops and disappears. When we did our boundary setting thing we never finished it but it didn't seem to matter"* (R, July 2006)

John had refused to prescribe boundaries, which was spot-on, and encouraged the team to decide on these boundaries themselves. However, because they were still refusing to take responsibility, they had not made a decision regarding the future direction and core values. To address continual requests for instructions on boundary setting, John issued a letter that read: **'This letter authorises you to do whatever you need to do (legally and ethically) to delight our customers and improve our business'**. Highly simplistic, almost crass, but it worked, and so began the process of 'letting go' and truly empowering the staff. It was also well received. SD's comments are typical of the impact on the workforce: *"We don't have to ask permission, if we know it's a good idea or that it will speed things up we can go for it! It only has to be little tiny things, but it will make things better."* (R July 2006)

During July 2005, the company was subjected to a financial audit from ELWa (a government funding body at the time). It was at this point that we all discovered just how poor the management and systems had been and this was, it turned out, the largest perturbation they were to suffer. This was partly the result of measuring activity. In addition to this, internal record keeping and quality systems, which had been linked to performance criteria and bonuses, were a shambles, according to John. Thankfully, the quality of the delivery was never in doubt.

As the company had taken a substantial knock as a result of the audit, I felt it was time to agitate things even further to push the company into a region of bounded instability. At another team meeting, we discussed what qualities (behaviours & skills) each member of the team required and how we might best evaluate them. It was decided to run an anonymous appraisal, where other team members, including the executive, appraised everyone else. This was a major turning point through which everyone, including John, learned a lot about themselves.

Following the appraisals, the results were collated and fed back to individuals in a private environment where they could discuss general feelings and some specifics. Alongside the quantitative results mentioned above, were open qualitative answers. It was the content of these fields that caused most concern amongst the team as personal comments were added. As a consequence, feelings were mixed and emotions ran high.

The main areas the company considered poor were:

- Communication
- Mixed attitudes
- Poor commitment to innovation
- Sharing information
- Sharing the goal.

Some took this as an opportunity to discuss shortcomings, especially John's communication and approachability, so that they could develop and take the team forward. Others, however, had been 'found out' and saw the whole process as a threat: *"He certainly took on the feedback from the questionnaires that went out, whether they were a success or failure, regardless, he took on board the comments and made himself more approachable."* (Team July 2006)

*"I knew that H and D and K were a waste of space; that they weren't doing their job and um…. and the other assessors knew that too - because obviously working as a whole they would know when people sloped off down the pub having a, you know,' late lunch' all day kind of thing. They knew that, they're not stupid, so I think that appraisal was kind of a way of everyone being honest and protected because a lot of people didn't have the b\*\*\*\*\*ks to go and say, ' I've got a problem with the way you're working'. No-one really had the balls to say that to anyone.   There wasn't that kind of openness before …"* (Interview RS2)

The outcome was interesting and unexpected given that this was about empowering the individual. One person, who had come out on top, gained so much self-confidence that she applied for a job elsewhere, which was not a great outcome to be honest! Some of those who had been 'found out' as under-performing and as having a bad attitude chose to leave, again not really the purpose of this process.  One person argued that the perception of his effort was wrong and made attempts to correct it, but within two weeks had reverted to the poor performance stated by his colleagues.  He left to pursue a career elsewhere. This is an example of self-organisation, which is unpredictable and emergent.

John was left with a smaller, but more committed bunch. As John and I had forced the team into an area of bounded instability, the next step was to facilitate the creation of connectivity and to get them fully involved in addressing the problems that had been identified at the audit.

Communication (especially from the leader, John) had been highlighted as a problem so we began again to discuss ways of improving the situation in an open and honest fashion. It was up to John to admit faults and accept criticisms to prove how committed he was to putting things right. John also took steps to increase the chances of communication by immediately issuing everyone with a mobile phone and setting up weekly communication meetings.

*"We've all got our phones. We didn't all have the phones before and some people didn't like using their own phones, but we've all got the phones now so we can say when anybody starts work here, 'If there's something you don't know about ask someone – don't try and struggle away and get it wrong because you don't know, just ask'. It has certainly made it a lot easier, I mean B phones me up at least once a day so that's showing how it's worked"* (R July 2006)

The communication meetings began in September, when two strategic teams were self-elected to improve quality and performance. Everyone was in fairness given the opportunity to contribute and to be involved in one or both of the teams. There were complaints of excessive workloads and demands for payment for 'extra' duties as involvement responsibilities were appreciated. The team was now in a state far-from-equilibrium, in the term 'chaotic order'. The challenge was to keep them there without reverting to the old control mechanisms of negative feedback established and reinforced for sometime, a little by John and a lot by his colleague. It was also important to stay close to the team to evaluate the tension and stress levels.

*"Chaos can be a positive thing because it pushes people to do things they wouldn't think about doing or would not have done in the past; it's a sort of development thing. Chaos and stress can, at times, be good for you. It's not always negative. Although there's been chaos it's been quite challenging. It*

*would be good for T2 to look and see where we are now. They are very targeted with NVQ's on point systems where you have to get points in at the end of the month. If I went back to that now I'd really struggle."* (B July 2006)

By early October, John was enthused by the emergence of connectivity. This was confirmed when John was approached by two of the more inexperienced staff who were concerned about their involvement in the performance and quality teams. Their concern was that they were getting involved in areas that they were uncertain of; when they still hadn't really, in their view, mastered their own jobs. The comments from R & B confirm the new levels of connectivity:

*"Everyone understands that each one of the workforce is equally important and everyone knows what everyone else does. When you take the hierarchy away it's not a case of just taking away managers, it's about bringing everyone's importance level up. But some people want to be more important than others and crave a job title to prove it. We haven't got room for that."* (R, July 2006)

*"Where I am now I can see my impact on the business, whereas with my previous employer I was just one of thousands. If I was off work now for any reason, I would see the impact that would have, my contribution is vital, and that makes you feel valued. Before I didn't feel that. If you were off they'd just keep going as though it didn't matter if you were at work or not. Now it's completely different. You have to work together to keep the money coming in."* (B, July 2006)

This was the first time John had been challenged and it proved that he had to let go of control more than he had ever done before, and start the process of leadership via democracy, values and nudges. John had to give them the option to contribute or not to contribute and, although he believed it was good to involve people, this had to be assessed and implemented individually. It was not a case of one size fits all, which again John grasped enthusiastically as there was a hint of self-reflection in what made him start his own company and, more importantly, motivated him.

*"There could be too much responsibility and then that would cause pressure and pressure is not a good thing … sometimes because it can be turned into a negative and because you kind of run away from it – the pressure. You don't have to take this pressure, do you? But you are taking it all on board, so the fact that it could be pressurised means that you could run away from it and no-one is telling you that you can't run away from it, so you do. There is no-one controlling it."* (B, Secondary Research Oct 2005)

By the end of August, they had agreed that the co-director would leave the business in November. So, during October 2005 he interviewed a number of staff to gather evidence for his dissertation on this same subject. It is extremely interesting to compare the interviews information/data with the interviews conducted by myself in August 2006 as part of my intervention. The general attitude within the team around that time largely centred around a reluctance to take responsibility without additional payment, the fear of risk-taking and of the blame culture which had developed within the peer group.

These lovely chaps above are John Ward, John Batten and Dr
Paul. Chicago 2007.

# Chapter 6
# Connectivity & Emergence in action
## Observation comments from team meetings.

In the follow-up research John's company started to grow and prosper. 'JS', one of the newer staff, had now emerged as quite a keen leader in developing the new processes and procedures required to take them forward in the coming year. During one of the meetings it became quite clear that degrees of connectivity and interdependence were improving as people were far more open and trusting. There were now people who were keen to get involved in this process, and they were now speaking out, whereas in the past they hadn't. In particular, the new staff, X and Y, were taking a leading part in voicing their opinions and bringing good ideas to the team. With this being a Performance and Training (PAT) meeting it was obvious that they had to address very important areas such as targets and performance, especially in new starts, over that period. During the process it became quite obvious that the team had finally grasped the importance of the targets set by ELWa.

*"I think the biggest change is in how people react with having the freedom to control what they do. We all know what we've got to do; we all know the figures the government hold above our heads and things like that. So everybody knows what they've got to do and they have the freedom to say 'right I've got it, this is my pile of candidates, this is what I've got to do, how I do it is pretty much up to me."* (R, July2006)

In November 2005 we saw the departure of the director and the ex-general manager. These actions caused further instability as the remaining team members questioned their departure.

*"To begin with they freaked! All of a sudden the person who had been accountable for them and who took the blame, was no longer there. Now they were accountable for themselves and I think because everyone – I'm not saying the team we have now, but certainly the team we had before – were very much into the blame culture. That meant that if they f\*\*\*\*d up then that didn't matter because E would get it in the neck, it was E's responsibility to make sure they were doing their job."* Interview RS3

Open and honest communication in the form of explanation and discussion reduced the tension. Most saw it as an opportunity to move on positively:

*"It was great to me because I could just get on to do what I needed to do."* (J, July 2006)

*"No-one was scared to ask questions anymore. Not scared, that's not the right word ... no-one had any reservations about asking questions I don't think anybody cares about feeling stupid by not knowing anymore. I think there was a bit of 'I better not ask that just in case somebody thinks I'm an idiot', before. Nobody cares about that [anymore]."* (R, July 2006)

In November, further quality problems meant the company lost 'direct claims', which meant that there would be a delay of up to five months in us receiving payment for work carried out.  This put further demands on staff, cash flow and profit.

*"Those that hadn't been here very long didn't quite know what it meant.  But once you explained exactly what it meant and the people thought about it..."* (R, July 2006)

*"It knocks your confidence because you had thought you were doing everything OK.  From my perception, realising everything was all wrong and could be better ... it made you think, what was going on?  It went downhill from there.  We started to put processes in place and things started to improve. That was a low point.  When staff left that was a bit scary too, with so many candidates and not enough assessors, but it has improved."* (B, July 2006)

John recognised that it was now time to step back in and lead the rebuilding of confidence and energise his leadership role within the company.  Somehow, John had to get them to understand where the company came from and reassert his passion. So, he took them into a completely empty room, to represent the position were he started five years previously, and he then explained his ethos, values, passions, desires and ideas in life, as well as in the company, to offer them his trust and respect and asked them to speak openly about their experiences.  John was surprised as he was met with a very positive attitude and comments:

*"You should have done that ages ago, now we know where you are coming from! Everyone values their job and appreciates the business's needs and everyone is working to their times.  S pops in frequently, which shows she's not skiving and appreciates the flexibility.  Everyone is the same.  Before I thought it was stupid, because I knew people would go home at*

*different times, but that's where you learn. It's the environment and the trust from the people we work with, and the trust and flexibility you give us. You get more out of your staff that way because they're comfortable and happy, not de-motivated."* (L, July 2004)

*"You've got more of a self-thing. I have my own personal targets which I want to hit and tick-lists which I do for myself, and if I don't achieve that I'll be gutted. I'm setting myself targets which are achievable whereas before I knew they weren't achievable."* (B, July 2006)

The meeting began the real process of underpinning the foundations of much better relationships, trust and connectivity with all staff, and continued discussion of what they stood for as a group ... adding value to clients' work. The main theme that came from the meeting was that, despite the problems they had been through, the value the team was most committed to was 'quality'. The group discussed what we represent and what our culture was and should be, with me facilitating. As Stacey (1992) says, '(culture) cannot be imposed from outside, even by top management.'

All people were viewed by the John as equally important to the team and were given equal support. This was a fact confirmed by the people who were interviewed.

*"Everyone here has an equal chance, we are all encouraged to improve and John recognises we may need different levels of support and we get just that. It's great working here."* (IIP Report, 2006)

These foundations were built on further over the coming months with regular weekly meetings. Additionally, John and I made ourselves available for any ad-hoc discussions. The quality and performance teams had been working together to look at flexible alternative ways forward. They had individually and collectively volunteered to examine the 'ELWa Specification' in minute detail to enable them to rewrite our policies and procedures around our agreed 'purpose' that the team had developed: 'To deliver training to learners in a way that is acceptable to the individual, within boundaries set by funding bodies, and with the highest regard for quality'.

R makes a comment about targets and knowing one's purpose:
*"You can still go and see the same number of people but what you do with them is different. You go and see those people and work with them instead of just going to see them and saying, 'sign this to prove I've been here'."* (R, July 2006)

People had started to take responsibility. B comments on trust and empowerment:
*"I'm not just an assessor, we start people up and try to sell the business and the NVQ's and get involved in presentations and meetings with the managers. Others in my old company wonder how I was able to get involved in that. Recently I went for lunch where the subject of changes in contract, and changing hours came up. I recounted the story of the mandate we had been given about being able to do whatever we wanted to do as long as it improved the business. My old colleagues said 'what?' – and they were laughing. I explained that I could make a decision and not have to check it with John as along as we felt it would benefit the business. They said 'what if it goes wrong?' I*

*said, if it goes wrong it goes wrong! They were gob-smacked to be honest. To me, it's their work that's completely mental, even though I used to work like that."* (B, July 2006)

*"I haven't got to ask for anyone's permission to do anything which is great for me because I can just get on and do something and if a decision needs to be made I can make it there and then. When you're left to your own devices you can manage your own workload and you know what time you're going to have available to deal with any issues"* (J, July 2006)

*Their investment in people is part of the ethos of the organisation where he (CEO) believes that the people are the heart of the business. To allow his removal of control over people he has had to ensure that people are encouraged to provide their ideas, that they are supported appropriately, and that they are developed to undertake their role.* (IIP Report, 2006, 10.1)

Now that communication was finally improving in the company, the team decided that activity targeting was counterproductive and that forecasting was about as accurate as reading tea leaves. So the company adopted a more mature way of thinking based on our 'the reason of being here' approach. The role of the quality team was to work on the systems to enable staff to achieve greater results.

*"There are systems in place with the forms ready to go, which is good for me, and we've got LJ checking the progress reviews. We could improve on forms going missing that I know I've handed in. Maybe a filing system, or signing for things when we hand things in? Then when I ask for help or support they will often try their best. There is support there and if I'm stuck I*

*just phone or ask and they'll answer straight away, there's never a delay."* (B, July 2006)

Unfortunately, one assessor, who had struggled with the company's leadership approach and felt stressed by the additional responsibilities, opted to leave the company all together, stating that she needed structure, targets and a 'boss'. She re-joined the company six weeks later, having experienced all of her list and thought differently, and fitted well into the mindset.

It is so surprising to me and John that this happens so frequently. Not leaving the company, but the failure to notice the changes within themselves, the freedom that comes with Simplexity. Leadership/Culture, and how it's impossible to revert back once you have experienced this way of doing things.

B commenting on how she discusses work culture at WhichWay with ex-work colleagues:

*"They think it's another world and don't understand. They say, 'what are your targets'? and I say there are no targets! They don't know how you achieve things, and I try to explain that you talk to people, share information and you get out what you put in. But I understand why they don't get it, because I was there myself. You're being brainwashed into a way of working in that type of environment. They see it as everybody having to hit targets, to make money. You'd spend two weeks every month giving people a one-to-one, which is two weeks time gone. You could have used the time to strengthen their ability by giving them extra coaching or support to achieve targets, but you knew it had to be done, so you'd just sit there and chat."*

During meetings in January, there was another call for a co-ordinator to further improve systems in the way they operated, a hiring process which led to changes in our internal recruitment.

Over the years, they had evolved the internal recruitment process from simple interview to interview and presentation, and eventually to full assessment days. The incumbent staff had always had limited input into the process, which led to questions about the selection of certain individuals and of letting others in. This time it had to be different and better. Applicants were short-listed against requirements that had been drawn up by the team. Each team member, be they assessor, administrator, HR or Executive was encouraged to state his / her particular expectations of the candidate. This led to a loose 'recruitment specification' – John did not use job descriptions as he quite rightly believed that this limited the individual.

*"I know what my job is and it changes all the time. Job descriptions are limiting and can be a cop-out – 'it's not in my job description'. It's just the culture we have."* (R, July 2006)

Interviews were held and then, to the shock of the candidates, the final interview was held by representatives of the team (all were invited). John excused himself from this part of the process, leaving the staff to establish the boundaries. Finally, the team discussed the outcomes and made recommendations. It was interesting and encouraging to observe the depth to which they had questioned the candidates and the conclusions they had reached. It was important that John went with the team decision, which he did, but also facilitated the exploration of all avenues along the boundaries of the company. The result was that on day one our new operations leader knew everyone, how they thought, how they worked, and they knew her. Within a few hours it was as if she had been there for months. The team was very pleased with their decision and it greatly improved both their communication and performance.

*"Everybody knew what she was about before she started. Everyone accepted her because there weren't any surprises and she came in and just started work."* (R, July 2006)

John became more and more surprised by the mindsets, behaviours and actions of the team as a whole, and company performance. The degree of communication and connectivity improved significantly and everyone was very happy in their roles. Staff members were excited coming to work.

*"It's a happier place to work in and to be able to talk to people openly rather than all the whispering that went on."* (B, July 2006)

*"It has taken a long time for people to actually realise that they can be honest with each other and can be open. I think when you've worked in environments that you have to answer to people, you get a rollicking if you bring bad news!"* (J, July 2006)

Results took a long time to manifest themselves, as so many mistakes had been made. However, the performance statistics rocketed and the company now exceed all but one of DELL's (formerly ELWa) performance targets. Staff took on the responsibility of liaising with assessors, rectifying shortcomings and developing new systems, which enabled them to regain 'direct claims'. Previously, they would have battled to get this done, and even then it would probably have been done very reluctantly.

*"It was a miracle. We all pulled together and worked out what needed to be done and got on with it. It was hard with no claims ...but we all did a bit of it to try and work out what we had to do, working out the tech certs, trying to get different processes formed. We had help from D, which was good. If you buried your head in the sand it would have such an impact on the business."* (B, July 2006)

Since the team evolved from a bitter, badly connected group of individuals into an empowered, engaged and well-connected team, they have been rewarded with some notable achievements. These are accomplishments, which John states could not have been attained without their commitment:

- Health & Safety score rose two points.
- Direct claims status replaced
- Successful LSC audit
- Outstanding IIP recognition

All staff stated they are happy and wouldn't want to work anywhere else. The conclusion of IIP confirms that:

*'[WhichWay] had achieved what many organisations look for; people genuinely believed in the organisation and felt it was 'their' business and not just an employer. This is a great compliment to the Director and the people at WhichWay Solutions'.*

Leaders need to consider all of the catalysts that encourage achievement of equity. They need to be brave and remove hierarchy. Simplexity is not a simple 'seven step' tool to be introduced by 'tool heads' but a way of thinking, a way of acting and more importantly, as John proved, a way of doing.

I think it fitting that I should leave the last comment to John:

*The main downfall of my approach to this process initially was to introduce Complexity? and expect people to readily accept it, and for it to work without any further input. It was by further study of the work of Mitleton-Kelly (2003), Lewin (1993) and Stacey (1992), that I realised how wrongly I had approached this subject Indeed, it was only by increasing my connection with Dr Paul that I started to grasp I was part of the system, and could not step back. I was the energy, leadership*

**John Ward**

*and values which started the company in the first place. As Mitleton-Kelly states, one cannot stand back and wait for the right solutions to emerge, as I initially did. I soon learned that I had to establish a new style of leadership in WhichWay that would strongly influence what emerged in terms of mindset, creativity, and adaptability. This means challenging and, if need be, removing conflicting leadership styles at management levels.*

*My leadership style has become a combination of all of the above; releasing control, offering trust (not expecting it to be earned), encouraging extremely high levels of communication (of the good and the bad) including financial information, allowing decision making, encouraging risk-taking, eliminating fear of failure and asking why – three times. One technique used (although this technique is long-term and risky) is to refuse to make decisions. This encourages wider thinking, more open discussion and generates more ideas – which enables more valuable input and grows the individual.*

# Chapter 7
## New Leaders, Changing Future – Must-do-list

In the beginning of my book I tackled the need to remove management (the thing not the people) and why now, this is more important than ever.

Those who have, until quite recently, advocated the need for more managers, more control and tighter rules on the workforce must now surely be feeling regret. Even now, some organisational managers still think that in, for example, a recession – and for the most part public services are always in a recession with year-on-year cutbacks – to survive we must retrench into what we see as safe and what we are most familiar with. Yet, it is quite apparent that if you rely on quality, or cost, or price, you will not survive because everyone is relying on one, two, or all three of these elements. Only now are managers starting to realise that in these tough times it's the frontline workers who add value and this includes quality, cost reductions, and price advantages, and that 'X-factor' which guarantees loyal customers and valuable innovation.

DNA, has stated for several years, way back in 1999, that our notion of work is based on out-dated assumptions of what work looks like – a vision that simply does not apply in a globally affected economy, where 24/7 operations are the norm. We are, in fact, still using 19th century management and organisational thinking applied to 21st century companies. We are now seeing the first signs of businesses who treat their workers like children, telling them what, where and how to work ... and then policing their every move,

and in the process getting into real difficulty. Are you one of them? No? Then just ask your staff honestly if they feel excited driving into work everyday? I suspect the answer will be no, and if it is then I'm afraid you need to change.

My research has shown clear links to poor management and a failure to engage staff as the first symptom of a struggling organisation. Bottom-up transformation is now understood as the only way forward and if this is accepted, then the rarefied strata of managers, large salaries and executive perks will soon disappear, to be replaced by warm leaders, perhaps on equally money not more, as a result of the extra efforts needed in the dawning of the age of the 'mess' and human complexity.

Impossible? Not so! Companies around the world work to a model of 'democratic leadership', such as Best Buys (USA) and Semco (Brazil), with even IBM designing its work practice around the views of its 140,000 workers in a global on-line chat, led and designed by the staff themselves. For we now have 'knowledgeable workers', who may not be fully 'academic' with reams of qualifications, but are nonetheless able to critique a process, innovate, and add value for customers. But, these are businesses, commercially driven, profit valued companies, not social companies such as NHS service, I hear you say, and you are quite correct. However, you are missing the point if you simply use this argument to dismiss the significance it could have on leadership in public or voluntary services.

Public services are primarily people based. People, customers, clients are individuals and bring with them a unique mess, a mess which can only be dealt with properly by free thinking, passionate professionals, who are flexible within the core values of the organisation. Core values, such as safety, cost, fun, friendly atmosphere, etc. establish boundaries within which the employee/professional is free to operate. Most organisations fail to create values, relying on vision, or rules, or procedures that never work unless the value hidden in them is explained and exposed.

Even customers, as a result of an availability of information, will understand values, or the lack of them, and will want to know where their coffee is from, who's making it, and at what cost? They will communicate with others about your service (or lack of it), and may even be able to leave comments and feedback on websites, free from the control of their service provider. You only have to look at websites detailing the 'user experiences' on various sites to understand that the power is not with marketeers or managers, but with consumers of the service and with the frontline staff. This consumer knowledge also includes, of course, what your competitors are doing as well.

Public Services simply cannot say one thing and do another. Nostalgia and basking in the warm glow of past customer loyalty will not save a company as ably demonstrated by Woolworths, a UK company started in 1909 that people loved, yet never frequented. It ceased trading in 2009!

UK workers have demonstrated time and time again that they are up there with the best. This is despite the woeful lack of investment in staff training in the UK. What training is available is often more to do with the 'how' they do what they do, rather than 'why' they do it that way. You only have to look at Japanese owned and managed companies here in the UK to see that workers increase output by eighty per cent more than anything achieved under a UK management style. And here is the sting: it's UK Management that's the problem not the solution.

**In order to survive a crisis my tips are as follows:**

1. Establish a **clear understanding** of what each department/section/person does for the rest of the organisation. Then ask simply, 'How does this knowledge of each person's contribution help our current customers and gain us new customers?'
My research indicates that the problem could lie with managers assuming they have to control others, even though they admit they don't have control over their own children! With this perception, many will quickly forget what they are there for, and indeed will not even care why they are there. Establishing communication without titles will re-establish core values and focus on customer needs.

2. Create **truly flexible areas** of work, where team members can sit and work together, outside of 'formal' teams/roles. What we need in times of high pressure and stress is to be able to rely on real flexibility from all staff. Flexible staff create mutual trust as everyone needs to talk and

communicate about what they are doing. By doing this, new meaning, understanding and co-operation increases. Then remove the break-time, lunch-time, sickness policies and all other petty rules. Throw them all out and put the people who make them back on the frontline so they can add real value. Many policies are not legal requirements or government regulations; most have just accumulated over time and over years of managerial power- seeking. It's people and customers that make the place work and survive - not policies or rules.

3. **Create a 'Knowledge Pub'** – an informal relaxation area to have 'me-time' and 'team-time'. With increasing stresses from the external environment it has never been more important to have time, space and the ability to communicate informally. Informal 'rest' times are the most productive ways of re-energising staff, removing damaging stress/worry and allowing greater effectiveness.

We are not machines, and allowing people to exchange information when they want to rather than when they have to will increase your company's rate of innovation, effectiveness and sustainability. Try one afternoon a week, where staff just create new ways of doing things better... start small and build.

4. Have **opt-in projects** where at least one administration officer and 'other team member' become involved. It's important to de-layer, but not in real terms of getting rid of staff, but rather by de-layering the nonsense of 'status', roles, and titles. More than ever we need a complete team approach, where the formal 'manager' is more often than not useless or out of their depth. If we have opt-in projects and think tanks it allows the formal leader to have input but from a less formal position. It is also a great way for others in the company to understand what's really going on.

Long-term sustainability and success will come from the frontline. It will be as a result of encouraging diversity, trust, empowerment, and, of course, democracy. Promoting leadership from the bottom will help everyone engage and deliver far more than in traditional top-down, manager led companies. The advantage is in the organisation. The solutions are already there in bucket-loads and no consultant will provide a tenth of the ideas that staff already have (if only they were asked) for saving money, and moving the company forward.

5. Have complete '**agile working**' and remove core hours. Flexible shifts, output driven.  Try and remove scheduled meetings, meet when important, not because you've a regular slot in the diary. We have been in a 24/7 culture for some years. Therefore, we need to lose the notion that we are buying time from workers. We are not. We need to buy talent.

Getting staff engaged means allowing them to take a little more control of how and what they want to do. Set the 'needs' of the company/service through open 'opt-in' debates and let them get on with it. Don't micro manage! Micro managing will only increase harmful stress levels for you and the workforce with the consequential poor results. Micro management also reduces the worker(s) to the five year old again as mentioned earlier. Trust that they will contribute when needed.

6. **Establish fun things** – starting with a quiz if you have to. How many people believe that work is fun? Usual answer – none!  Not a surprise as our research shows that most people believe that by definition work has to be drudgery, as otherwise it would be fun, and we don't get paid for having fun!

One startling result from our research was that employees feel that work is always unproductive, political and unfair. We at DNA feel that for managers and workers who don't come to understand that there is a reasonable, effective alternative to what they have known, change will be very painful. This pain can be avoided only if you allow for private and work life to merge.

7. Work on, and create, **positive** initiatives to challenge perceptions of downturn, crisis, stagnation, and managers as 'policing' people looking to catch people out, squeeze more from them, and stop them being managers. Ask them to be authentic, normal, people focused and more than anything a coevolved purpose.

8. Whiteboard to prepare work/projects and **allow open communication.** You must allow everyone, when possible, to contribute to ideas, direction and services. Even if they don't contribute, simply having the option to will increase participation, implementation and reduce resistance at a time when things need to be done quickly and without wasting resources, time or effort. Staff need to feel involved and able to have their say in an open, trusting environment. Doing this will also stop the whispering campaigns and destructive gossip that frequently damages companies.

9. **Reduce meetings** – and when they are held, include everyone, and, where possible, have open meetings. Keep meets to a maximum twenty minute duration for get-togethers. People at all levels of the organisation, but especially managers, must stop doing any activity that is a waste of work time, customers' time, or simply anything that does not add value. Writing policy or procedure is a good example – by the time they are written they are already out of date.

Ask yourself if writing them is the best way to  communicate purpose and value, and question why they are needed? Welsh Government, Wales, UK, is a prime example of poor structure, confused processes and misguided efforts. The drive to do things urgently to save Welsh Manufacturing is off-put by the need of the civil servants and politicians to protect their positions and minimise risks and comebacks. It has simply focused inwards and is not output driven in action.

10. Establish the concept that **'work+fun'** creates a better employee, more output, great job satisfaction and fewer negative issues. HR must lead by example! According to our on-going research, we need to let all employees have the freedom to work the way they want. If it's flexible working, then let it happen and do not check up on them or let only certain levels or departments do it, you will simply send out the clear message 'we don't trust you'! Companies must make work something they do, rather than a place they go. Stop talking about hours or clocking people in and ask instead for their commitment, their passion, and ideas on how to make things better, faster and more pleasing to the customer whilst reducing costs or/and increasing profits.

11. Become **Adults** & not Children ... ask **why x 3** ... as an adult, always look for a quicker, better, cheaper and more fun way of doing something. Think purpose from the mind set of the **'customer'** and you'll see immediate change.

Companies who champion democracy and equality in the workplace will be better placed to innovate, create and above all adapt to a rapidly changing market, a market from which suppliers and customers disappear almost daily.

Why? It's quite simple. Any business, large or small, private or public, that believes in values-led, people-first, will have all staff engaged, empowered and seeking new ways to survive, rather than a few, overpaid, over stressed managers trying to claim control of the organisation and market.

# Chapter 8
# Company Change


## Case Study:  AJM Sewing – 'The knickers factory'

There are no sensible M&S bras and knickers for this factory, its simply an amazing and exciting place where the women and men for that matter get excited. AJM produce the raunchiest of underwear for some of Britain's high-end lingerie retailers and are based in the most unglamorous place of New Tredegar (sorry people of New Tredegar) in the former industrial valleys of South Wales.  Yet, despite these big-name contracts, they were in 2010 struggling to keep their head above the financial waters. Owner, James Meller, openly admited he had had no formal management training and knew he could do with help to grow the company and make it sustainable. For me that was a rare and delightfully honest confession, which made James one of the best leaders and owners I've come across in terms of honest reflection, willingness and risk taking. With a recession looming, he knew he had to change, and change fast as the costs were quickly rising and the profits reducing.

So he called me to see if I could help. And it was only then – when I asked to see the books – that James admitted the extent of the problem. The company was £40,000 in the red and had been a few times in the past, rescued only by his father's cash investments. I was, however, confident that the company could survive; indeed it had to survive as the only seamstresses left in the Wales region and the skills itself were dying fast. It wasn't going to be easy and that became clear from the financial facts and a quick scan of research on knickers and sales, I'd have to change the mind-set of the factory's workforce.

The fact that James had no formal management training was in my eyes quite good. His passion was in the industry, the materials and fashion. Business skills can be taught. Passion cannot.

The rub here was that the forty machinists – mostly in their late fifties – had all been sewing since they were about fifteen years old and had seen a number of bigger companies like James that came and went. They'd done the rounds of the local sewing factories, always working in the same way, with a line, by line, mechanistic approach. AJM carried on the traditional mindset of this with the 'girls' working on a production line, with supervisors, a factory manager, and then the company boss.

So how were they going to take to my views that the factory would be better, not to mention profitable – if they ran it themselves? One worker, Denise, summed it up when she told James: *"I just want to come to work, do what I've got to do until four o'clock, then go home, shut the door and forget about it. If I was in charge, I wouldn't have clocking off. Nobody here is going to do that for £5.75 an hour."* And that was what James was up against.

I am used to opposition, resentment, fear and 'naysayers' at all levels, and I certainly got it at AJM! The machinists told him they didn't even want to see the company's books, let alone take responsibility for budgeting. They'd been working in the same way for forty years and they were not going to change now, and not even my boyish charm was going to shift the ladies. Retirement was tantalisingly close, and even the prospect of a share in the company's potential profits wasn't going to convince them to change.

The management was different. James impressed me because he turned out to be the first boss I had ever met who had ever admitted: *"I don't know what I'm doing here."* James actually *wanted* to hand over control to the workers, so he'd be freed up to be out and about, wooing new clients. And Yvonne, the factory manager at the time, wanted to retire shortly anyway, so both were keen to get involved in the system. She said she'd happily go earlier if I proved to her she really wasn't needed as manager, only advisor in the future. So the first meeting with management – James and Yvonne – was a walkover, the easiest I've ever experienced so far. I did at the time put this down to the fact James had grown up with the company and not had any formal training. He wasn't looking for status or power. He simply wanted success, fun and perhaps not to work so hard.

It was a different story with the staff. They mostly agreed with Denise that they didn't want to take on the responsibility of running the company. They said they knew how to sew – and that was about it. I told them if they could budget in their own homes, they could run the business. *"It's really not so complicated,"* I told them. *"And if you do this, it isn't more work for less money, it has freedom, fun and passion as the key reward. You could potentially be better off in all areas of life – and you'll certainly be happier, because you'll be able to do something about all those things that at the moment you just moan and groan about."*

Twenty minutes into the meeting however, there was trouble. The girls told me that there was management in the room and pointed out supervisor Tracy and office worker Debs, despite the fact that neither lady considered themselves management!    But the girls insisted they were, so I embarrassingly had to ask them to leave. I thought it was important to get the staff on their own, so they would be open and honest with me and they were. But by the end of the meeting, staff were still unconvinced, although some did start to speak up. They went back to their machines saying they'd listen again, but, really, they were sure that whatever I was thinking of implementing, *"wouldn't work here!"*

A week later I was back to talk to them again. This time James got the managers and the staff together. I have to say that looking back over the companies that have I worked with the thing that I failed at consistently was the impact or the momentum of impact, working as I did in the 'day job' of an academic; teaching, supervising researchers, and meetings, endless meetings in academia to prioritise the agenda of the next meeting. Honestly, the meetings culture was even worse than the increasing paperwork. Anyhow, my biggest weakness at the time was, well, time itself.

If truth be told, driving change, free of charge, alongside a full time job was extremely tough. The change here would have been much quicker and better if I could have worked there full time. But money, resources and a family to feed meant that this would have to be worked around until my theories/thinking could be proved as the future of organisations.

Anyhow, the girls asked me why I wanted to get rid of management, and just what that would mean for James and supervisor Tracy?

The turning point came when James told them just why he'd brought me in, and this was a shock to me as well as the girls. He explained how he felt he'd taken the company as far as he could, and needed some guidance on taking the factory – and all of them – forward. I told them it was even more basic than that – if they didn't change they wouldn't survive. I also reminded them that the UK was in a recession, that workers in China and India were taking British manufacturing jobs, and we had to change to stop this happening to this factory in New Tredegar, South Wales.

This time some of the staff left the meeting excited about the prospect of change. Supervisor Tracy said change was long overdue. Some of the girls were great, she said, but too many just didn't care – and she felt that this would sort the wheat from the chaff. They needed to take more responsibility, and if they thought something on the production line could be done better, they needed to speak up. While she tried to run things as well as she could, some things she just simply didn't see, so the more eyes focused on the goal of increased productivity, the better.

With the girls by and large wavering, but up for listening, I split them into groups and got them to list their complaints. Then, I got them to start changing things:

First – a morning coffee break. They'd always wanted a cuppa when they got to work, but James had insisted they got straight on the machines and cracked on. I gave them the green light to implement the break themselves – as long as they used it productively. They decided they'd have a coffee, but they'd ban talk of what happened on Corrie last night, and stick to discussions about what went well on the line yesterday and what the plans were for the coming working day.

Then they started to divide themselves into groups, so instead of one big linear set-up, they'd work in small teams. That meant physically changing the factory floor around and moving the machines.

Next they wanted to get rid of the bell that sounded at the start and end of breaks, and they also said they would like to be in a position to be choosier about the designers they worked with.

Now, after my visit, AJM are still in the midst of change, and the factory's future is still uncertain, but I remain confident that, if the workers remain passionate about what they do, they'll turn it around. I am now taking them to other factories which work this way to show them how their company could – and in my view should – be run. I am confident that if they carry on with the changes, AJM will be unrecognisable.

# Chapter 9
## JT Morgan.

This Swansea department store reached its ninetieth birthday in 2008, but at the start of the year it had fallen on hard times. The landmark shop went into administration, with eighty redundancies. Only twenty workers were kept on, but there was a glimmer of hope when the four former directors brought it back out of administration, with the promise of a move to a brand new shopping centre on the horizon.

Just weeks after buying it back, the directors agreed to meet me to see if I could help them. I had never been to the store, so first I visited as a 'mystery shopper' along with the BBC Radio Programme producer Gemma. I always attempt to view any company from a customer's perspective before starting work with the company, to see where exactly the problems lie – from the customer viewpoint if possible. This creates a fairly balanced first view of the organisation, before asking other customers what they think.

First impressions? *"Like something from Eastern Europe,"* was my conclusion. I was a bit shocked at the lack of stock, dreadful décor and confusing layout – not to mention the ladies fur coats, which had pride of place in the menswear department … at the height of summer! I was also taken aback at the lack of customers – and of staff. Indeed, on my second visit to the store, as I wandered the floors, it was twenty minutes before I saw anyone, staff or customer! So I suppose you could understand the need to bring me in, yep desperation.

Nevertheless, my first meeting with the four managers went well. They said they'd give my ideas a shot and agreed that I could meet their staff one day after work, in the shop's cafe. I did wonder how much they actually understood of my process and the commitment from them that would be needed. I commented after the first meeting that I would normally walk away from a company at this point if they were not truly committed to the process, and these four managers did not inspire confidence. The next stage for me, once the managers and seniors have agreed is to meet the people on-mass, to talk through what I am attempting to do, and more importantly what I am not doing. I do it together simply to stop the rumour mill, whispers and myths to arise. Its still happens, but at least I am seen to try at least.

The meeting with staff, normally quiet for the first meet, was more explosive than expected. No sooner had the managers left than the staff let rip. I normally have to coax staff to speak openly about the managers and to make them feel that they can trust me enough to say what they really think. On this occasion the frustrations, pain, anger just poured out. I heard how the staff had little faith in management, and how workers were feeling frightened and even bullied. Some had been there ten, twenty, or even thirty years, and by and large they'd all given up. Few thought the store would even make it to its new location.

I asked them if they could run the store better themselves. After all, between them they had centuries of retail experience! They did indeed have ideas for getting new suppliers and giving the customers what they really wanted.

This I suppose is the trick in all the companies I've changed the desire to make it work, the desperate need to prove the service, product can work and it can be successful. At the end of the meeting the staff seemed buoyed by my visit and were keen to meet me again. Then came the bombshell – they realised the managers were still in the building, and hadn't left, as the workers and I had thought. Many were afraid the managers would have heard what was said. What I didn't know at the time was that as a result of my meeting with the staff, the managers had decided to meet with each member of staff individually the very next day to question them. However, I didn't believe the staff when they said the managers were hiding around the corner in the stair well of the shop. I was even more flabbergasted when the staff were proved right.

But, whether they'd heard or not, the four directors agreed to meet me again. And this time there were real fireworks. One director threatened several times to walk out, shouting and swearing, and wagging his finger in my face. Even today if you listen to the radio programme you can hear the voice of one director so loud and clear as he ranted and this was because he was so close his voice was picked up by both his and my lapel microphones, he was that close! Several workers had told their managers what had been said in the staff meeting – not all of which was entirely accurate! They even accused me of de-motivating staff to a point that one had handed in her notice as a result.

By the end of the meeting, another director seemed to be coming around to my way of thinking and persuaded the others to meet up again the following week to show me the books, and thrash out some ideas. The director's comment was simple, *"Why wouldn't we want to take on Paul's ideas if the evidence suggests it works while all our own previous efforts had failed?"*

That meeting went much better than expected, and a couple of days later I was back in the store to meet the staff. This time, there was unrest. Over the course of the meeting, many of the workers walked out. They told me they didn't think I could make a difference to their company, and that they didn't want to know any more. I was also confronted with the accusation that what had been said at the first meeting had been 'made-up' and that any comments the workforce had made about the managers had been 'forced' out of them by my manipulation. I was shocked, and even though I had the transcript and recording from the first meeting, I didn't respond to their accusations but understood that they had obviously been 'threatened' by the managers into denying and retracting any negative comments.

That was the beginning of the end of my involvement. I believe in democracy, and I have to have the wholehearted cooperation from managers and staff to try to turn a company around.

But at all levels the people in this business had made it clear that they didn't want me there. Staff went to the directors and told them they just weren't interested. The directors told me they didn't think I should come back.

*"Do you think you have failed?"* one journalist asked.

*"No,"* I said, *"Because they didn't even listen – they didn't even begin to try out my ideas."*

In my world, that's not a failure, although a failure is okay if honest, as it shows I tried. If they'd listened, I firmly believe it would have worked; the staff were willing and able. Even

114

today I still feel that I could have made a huge difference to the shop and turned around JT Morgan's fortunes. If the managers had only listened, just a little, to staff, the turnaround would have truly amazed them all.

And the shop? It closed in October 2011, and all twenty staff are now out of a job.

# Chapter 10
# Removing Managers – A quick view

Imagine finding a magic formula to improve frontline public services, to make staff happier and more engaged, and save money too!

One council in Wales has done just that. But not through magic, a business model, framework or even a guru-led formula. In fact, according to me, the champion of the method they used, it's pure common sense – just ask the staff to solve things for you. And stop managing them. That was the 'spin' told to the newspapers, the BBC, and anyone who wanted to know about what I was about to try next – a public sector refuse collection department, where not a lot had changed over the past few decades. The relations between 'them and us' were at best strained and at worst hostile, and change meant 'cutbacks'.

Looking back, there was always the suspicion this was a set-up to fail – a way to prove that my belief in people, and my thinking the Simplexity way of thinking in practice could work anywhere, even on the bins.

When Blaenau Gwent County Borough Council (BGCBC), a small poorly performing authority in an Objective One funded area decided they needed a change of culture, they allowed me and the DNA team to have a go at changing the council's 'management'. As a BBC Wales business presenter, I managed to get the council to allow the cameras in to film the change process as we went from talking to the senior leaders to beginning the change itself in the Environmental department. I say me, but Gemma Collins the genius behind the BBC Radio Wales programmes on the same subject of change from the ground upwards via the frontline staff, was the main person to persuade the council, which is a major achievement in itself.

As an academic who works with organisations to try to change their mind-set away from a traditional top-down, command-and-control culture, urging them to replace that methodology to one of trust in their employees, Gemma  commented, *"Paul was looking at leadership in a much more radical way, talking about how the leadership skills of all staff should or could be displayed."* Mark McIntyre, the council's Head of Governance commented, *"It's not leadership as we traditionally understand it because it's not leadership targeted at existing leaders per se, it's developing the leadership capacities of all employees."*

But Mark McIntyre didn't have an easy job persuading the council to try it – perhaps because my catchphrase is that I want to get **rid of managers and create leaders!** *"It took me probably the best part of a year to convince the corporate management team to try it,"* said McIntyre.

At the same time there was a change of administration with Councillor Des Hillman, who now led the new independent coalition in 2009, showing a keen interest. *"We wanted to refresh the services, to meet needs more effectively, and we wanted to offer the chance to frontline staff to make a*

118

contribution – to make it better," he said. *"We wanted to see it through the eyes of the people right on the frontline. They're innovative; they know the quirks of the job. Officers were however much more wary of me and the change, but winning the top management team around with examples of where Paul's work had worked? in about ten sessions (2 hours long) helped tremendously."*

The then chief executive, and visionary, Robin Morrison added, *"We were really aware we needed to change – we are customer-driven, they wanted better and better services and we were faced with less and less money. Paul was offering a programme of change that had been traditionally only offered in the private sector. There was a lot of concern that this wasn't the normal way we did business."*

The first part of the programme was to rip up all strategy,

*Dr Paul and the Binmen*

do away with managers and make leaders, and then give the workforce free rein to design our service, from the clients upwards. For most organisations that would be worrying. But me this approach is essential if organisations are to compete – even survive – in the modern world.

I commented to the BBC at the time, *"We don't need old-fashioned, 19th century management principles, particularly in public services. By ridding the organisation of managers we have a far better service which gives you efficiency and reduces waste. It also releases talent – organisations are traditionally run in a way which stifles it."*

With a message like that to convey it was no wonder the rest of the Public Services shuddered and closed ranks, but I was on a mission and being honest was part of that mission. The council launched a pilot project with around sixty managers – a sort of damage limitation exercise up front, just in case, but I didn't mind that just as long as I was in and working away.

*"What we needed to do was make sure our senior managers were comfortable and weren't stopping at the headline message, which was about getting rid of all managers,"* said McIntyre. *"Understandably there would be huge resistance to that. But once they'd gone through the six-week course a lot of them said it was a no-brainer."* Mark was, as HR Director, taking a huge risk, both personally and in his professional career. If this was to go wrong Mark was the energy and passion behind the initiative as he simply 'got it' in terms of theory and change practice. So much so that the Chief Environmental Services Officer, Alan Reed, volunteered his department as the guinea pig for trying out the message on frontline staff. Alan stated at the time, *"I really understood what Paul was getting at. It was already happening in some small areas of my division, and I thought it would be interesting to try it in the bigger areas."*

So, in October 2009 I started work with the council's refuse, recycling and transport teams. It meant dawn meetings, six am most days with the bin men and recyclers in the depot canteen before their rounds, and days in the council garage getting to know the mechanics and their immediate managers.

The first task was to challenge them and gain their trust, so I got them to offload their moans and groans and unmet needs. Those are some of the little things they can change straight away. That allows them to think they're starting to take power and control of the organisation. That's when I know I have convinced them, when they can see little things happening, be it new equipment or even changes in shift patterns. For the mechanics, for example, it was simply to turn on the radio so they could work with music playing in the background.

One of the key objections I always face, regardless of context or sector, is the notion that managers are paid to make decisions, and that frontline staff believe they're not up to taking on more responsibility. Often, they simply don't want to, as the system creates a way that the decision is taken up by this fictional structure. There's always someone who says 'I just want to do nine-to-five and go home', but they quickly realise that in today's organisations there really is no room for that type of attitude. But there are also always natural leaders amongst the organisation, and they're the ones I have to identify. Once I've convinced them, they'll bring the rest along with them.

But it was far from plain sailing to get to that point. There was a deep mistrust of management's motives for bringing me in, and a suspicion that I was really there as an 'axe-man' which, as son of a union representative and grandson of Dai Fedder (Mines Federation Representative), couldn't have been further from the truth. Even though I came with a guarantee that, while some people's roles may change, there would be no job losses, the resistance remained.

*"It was difficult to start with, and I had staff knocking on my door on a daily, if not hourly, basis,"* said Reed. *"They were worried about losing their jobs, losing control, and being moved away from their normal role. They saw this as a cost-cutting and job-cutting exercise. I had to try to reassure them and guarantee that this was not about job cuts but about changing the way they worked and introducing a different mentality into the workplace."*

As the 'Business Doctor', who had successfully turned around twenty-six companies prior to this public sector venture, I found myself struggling to convince the refuse and recycling teams, and for that matter the mechanics, that they were capable of making many of the decisions their managers made for them. And then, suddenly, the transport staff seemed up for the challenge. Handed the power to make decisions, they did all the little things that seemed to spur them on. *"It was simply having a radio on,"* said one mechanic, *"That instantly created a better atmosphere. It hadn't been on before because management thought it was a luxury."* They also changed their own shift patterns and worked on ways to bring revenue into the garage by attracting outside business. They shared leadership on a weekly basis and quickly developed new ways of working to improve not just their environment but also customer experience. One customer on the third day of the mechanics running themselves commented not only that everyone seemed 'happier' but, the service was greatly improved. All this and only three days into the change process.

With refuse and recycling it was a harder task. Because the staff were only in the depot for five minutes at the start and end of their shift it was really hard to engage them. They would come in, avoid me and drive off! Even in meetings I had no impact because the different crews didn't communicate with each other outside. They'd jump in their trucks, decide I was wrong, and the following day I'd have to start again. It was like Groundhog Day. It was really tough. I can, to this day, smell a refuse collection truck from miles away and recognise the distinctive noise of the engines!

But over the coming months I gradually won the crews round. I won't go into the specific details, but it involved constant arguments, threats of being beaten-up and at one point even my car was damaged. They did not, however, know the level of stubbornness I had, which was driven from the simple fact I knew that if they would only listen and have a go, the place of work would be much better. All their frustrations, and unmet needs over the decades could be dissolved in days and the council's need for savings would happen without job losses.

The council had a team of office staff working on initiatives to improve recycling rates and so reduce landfill costs. Recycling crews started approaching the team with ideas, and this was a key turning point for one part of the service. One crew took to knocking on doors, after work and in their own time, and showing people how to line food waste caddies with newspaper if they didn't want to buy liners – such was the level of their passion. Others visited schools and got children designing new signage for their lorries.

Refuse and recycling teams are on a 'job-and-finish arrangement', and many crews would head home shortly after lunchtime, despite being paid until four pm. *"Now, just a month into the change, many are voluntarily staying on,"* said

Alan Reed, *"When the recycling teams finish their rounds they're going around knocking doors, talking to residents, asking them if they recycle and, if they do, giving them a letter thanking them.*

*To me, that's ownership and taking control. We've tried to promote services with leaflets or even people in a shirt and tie*

*knocking the door, but it doesn't get the message across. You can tell people about European targets but they aren't interested. What better message can you have than the boys who collect your recycling knocking your door and saying, 'This is my job, and I want to do it'?"*

The Recycling crews moved the recycling rates of households from nineteen per cent to forty-one per cent in six months, without penalties or changes introduced. Amazing!

Some of the bin-men came forward to take care of administrative work before and after their rounds, and when one middle manager resigned to work elsewhere, his staff decided jointly with Reed that his role wouldn't be filled. Instead, his work was redistributed and his salary costs ploughed back into the service.

In the garage, there was a similar story as the staff nominated a mechanic to take care of paperwork and agreed a pay rise for him.

After a slow start among some of the staff, Alan Reed is in awe of the results he's now seeing. *"Some sort of realisation has hit the staff – that they can be in charge of their own destiny here,"* he said. The facts speak for themselves – sickness has decreased by five per cent, recycling and food waste tonnage is up, and £800k plus has been saved in staff and facilities costs. And, ninety-two percent of staff said the service was better as a result of the changes.

There was no hefty consultant's fee to pay either. As my work formed part of the on-going research, my services came free. The real reason was simple. The method – my method – was untested in Public Services, so how could I charge for such a risky process? In hindsight, I should have charged, as not charging simply places the process in a 'can't be good' mindset with the clients. The council members themselves were a pretty shoddy bunch and they soon started to use the changes as ways to score political points, with me as the football, and not one ever, privately or publicly, said thank you to me, the team or the crews themselves. Shameful behaviour that will remain in my psyche for years to come. It also taught me an important lesson in local council politics. Sometimes the goal to improve services is not the main focus of elected members, it's simply to get re-elected for another four years. Not all authorities are like this, and, indeed, through meeting the members of the neighbouring authority of Monmouthshire, my faith in publicly elected members was resorted.

"The HR Department commented, *"We recognised that some people's roles would change",* said Mark McIntyre, Director of Human Resources. *"This programme acted as the catalyst for some of those changes, but it was not the reason for them."* Now, other councils are evaluating the programme around the UK and beyond, with recent requests for his? work from as far afield as India. So there has been a tremendous energy created as a result of the work.

So what messages do those involved have for other public services facing changes?

*"Don't cut back the way you traditionally would."*

*"Don't slash the frontline or outsource the council services. That's just tinkering with a broken engine. You have to get at the hub of it and consult from the workers up. They will reduce so much waste and still provide a damned good service."*

*"Put in this thing called 'trust' and stop measuring, monitoring and policing everything."* Council leader Des Hillman said: *"Don't be afraid of having a go. The benefits can be very positive for the wellbeing of staff and for the efficiency of the service."*

But Mark McIntyre, the driving force behind this in Blaenau Gwent, has a word of warning: *"In hindsight, we should have spent more time making clear what it was we were trying to do. It shouldn't have been seen as a threat to managers or staff. At the heart of this is establishing and building on the team, and team support."*

## Rubbish! It's all just a load of old Rubbish
### An Insight into the BBC documentary " [Be] the Boss"

As described in the previous chapter, in 2008 I started working with Blaenau Gwent County Borough Council, a small south Wales Local Council, for over two years when the CEO at the time, Robin Morrison, via an old colleague invited me to talk to the Corporate Management team plus a few Human

Resource staff. The reason for the invite was that having performed 'poorly' in the recent past BGCBC, they? were actively seeking to change the way Public Services operated in their communities, whilst maintaining services with ever decreasing finances in Local Government provision and Welsh Government Assembly Support. The theory, tried and tested in over 25 small, medium and large businesses, based on the principles of Simplexity Thinking, had never really been tried in Public Services completely and this could be the place we help achieve results or fail miserably. These 'results' included increasing democracy by adding a real voice to the frontline (and not via Unions who I have seen do more harm than good), removing the waste in systems, by which I mean the daft stuff such as KPI's, needless reports, outdated procedures, and release staff to do things their way, so developing a culture and mindset of 'ownership'. This programme was never about the removal of managers (people) but the change from management to leadership, allowing management to be done by frontline staff.

In simple terms it helped understand the notion that organisations are about people; people are messy, subjective and individual and the more management you do the more cost you add to the organisation (and, the more importantly for me) the more you stifle the ability of the people within to do the job they do best. Moving from this idea of Management and Leadership as control and structure, to one which is about people, dealing with mess, understanding we don't all see it 'one-way' and if we treat people with respect and deference, we get a better place to live and work. The message from all this was again quite straight forward - Good leaders, and the removal of this traditional management notion, create and allow for passion and trust and need not rely on the formal system to achieve great things.

Before the change process and intervention began at all case studies, a research questionnaire and a series of 'random' interviews with all staff (then management, line supervisors and frontline) were conducted by external researchers.

The results in Blaenau Gwent County Borough (BGCBC) were quite startling but no different from many other organisations.

As an example of this, staff were asked:
'Do You Trust Management?' - and 94%, responded negatively to this question with 78% feeling they lacked any power to complete things in their daily role.
More importantly, the question, 'Are you in a trusted workplace?' resulted in 98% responding negatively. It will become clearer as to why this was significant with change in BGCBC later in this case overview.

It's important to note here that the dislike for 'management tools or 'theory' is not out of the ordinary as many have written about its flaws in present day application.

The skill of Management can cause much unhappiness in organisations through a focus on targets and measurement, control, organising others, with an absence of critical thinking skills, and a lack of human systems. There are exceptions, but these managers (aka leaders) are rare and usually eventually 'conform' to the world of mechanics, cogs, targets and measurement. This in part destroys the natural fabric of human creativity, innovation, trust, openness, ownership, inspiration and leadership as seen throughout my work and in many others. We are simply different, each one of us is an individual with our own ways of thinking and doing. The work of DNA Definitive attempts to realise this human potential and the development of an organisational architecture which accepts that direction, structure and influence are needed in the organisation without causing harm to the soft-systems within.

**In short**, DNA through the application of Simplexity Theory, helped to move the 4250 staff in the Blaenau Gwent CBC, and more specifically the 1200 Environmental Division which deals with Highways, Refuse and Recycling, Litter-picking, cemeteries, Contact Centre and Street Cleansing beyond focusing on targets and measures of effectiveness, away from performance management, control, them-and-us mindset and get them instead to focus on core values and boundaries that really matter for organisational sustainability.

The change began in BGCBC with all the Senior Managers taking part in 'Critical' Thinking seminars, which attempted to 'deconstruct' current thinking and practice in a 'safe' comfortable environment. It also allowed the managers to conceive the idea of taking public sector management to this place called 'leadership' (but not in the conventional sense). Leadership for this study revolves around 'individual values', co-evolution, connectivity, emergence, ideas, direction, subjectivity, mess and has more to do with inspiring and influencing people as to direction and values than with day-to-day implementation. This is simply left to the experts – the frontline staff. The 'democratic leaders' in this work, are throughout the organisation and are capable of influencing other people to do things without actually sitting on top of them with a checklist. But all this requires trust, openness, communication, risk and creativity, which are founded on the leaders being from within the social network of the organisation. Leaders in my companies are within and throughout the organisation and the resultant democratic processes inspire confidence in others and ourselves and as a result, we become more relaxed, communicative and successful (whatever this means for the organisation or department).

**Part two** of this work was about changing the mindset of the workforce. From one of subservience to ownership; from a blaming culture to one of responsibility; from the individual to the networked. This is where the 'Trust' or lack of it for the Bin-men, highlighted in the pre-survey caused so much difficultly. The bin-men saw management, 'innovations', 'new ideas' and cost-cutting, job losses and more-work-for-less and didn't trust me or for that matter the BBC film crew who followed their steps closely. For any employees to take increased ownership and personal responsibility for moving the organisation forward, employees require support, respect, trust, open communication, and opportunities. They have to network and communicate far more than is currently realised. However, with change comes risk and uncertainty, and the biggest challenge is the acceptance that uncertainty is a natural part of the process. For example, inspiring frontline staff to choose their staff uniforms, or arrange shift-patterns, or order equipment, gradually increasing responsibility.

Naturally, self-organisation and self-leadership will start to unfold, as other questions will begin to be raised.

Okay enough of the same case I know…. I just want you to understand the huge risk this intervention was in terms of career, money, theory, health, reputation and of course the DNA project itself.

### So the outcomes were?

The successes are always different in each division, organisation, department and these are always stated, as 'successes' by the frontline staff themselves, no manager states what s/he wants from the outset. The job and finish? for the bin-men and now all the workers still remains, yet they now work on average 7.4 hours per day, not 3.5 hours as previously. The idea of this is we buy talent and outcomes (note here not output) and not time. If we maintain the same 'managerial ideals' systems, thought processes, then yes the increasing burden on the men would result in a decrease of the value in wages, but this doesn't happen. Why? Well it's quite simple: in most organisations we throw out all of the systems, processes, rules, regulations (even Health & Safety to begin with!) and rebuild them from the service/product, back up the structure (or in my world down). The Bin-men are released from, for example, filling in 5 forms before they leave each morning to one simple checklist. One manager left during the programme for a new post outside the authority and wasn't replaced, which wasn't shown on the documentary at all, yet was a significant leap of faith in the frontline leadership. The crews and office decided that the role could be broken up and given to all the staff, saving around £120k per year with on-costs. His salary was used in part to hire 2 full time letter wardens later on post-programme. Although a little was used to pay the frontline staff a little more in hourly rates, but this was to equal out injustices in the pay scales.

There were no 'managers' left in Environmental Services, only Leaders, and they change according to experience, responsibility, project and needs of customers and Councillors, voted in as and when needed by the staff themselves. The money saved by this experiment , estimated to be in excess of £900k was/is being invested for the most part back into frontline services, decided by the staff themselves. This fact was mentioned in the Audit Commission Report 2010 and Western Mail 2011.

http://www.wao.gov.uk/assets/Local_Reports/Blaenau_Gwent_Council_Corporate_Assessment_English_Updated.pdf (point 57)

http://www.walesonline.co.uk/news/south-wales-news/blaenau-gwent/2011/05/12/blaenau-gwent-council-learn-lessons-from-ban-the-boss-series-91466-28668527/

http://www.walesonline.co.uk/news/south-wales-news/blaenau-gwent/2012/01/05/council-takes-steps-to-be-more-agile-91466-30060160/

It's also worth noting here that the Bin-men and the 'bosses' were the product of the Council system. They have behaved and acted this way, I suppose, simply as that was what the system expected. They are the product of the way the organisation was socially constructed and structured. They were/are not naturally managers, they became managers because the organisation expected them to and indeed the staff wanted it. They saw only one way of organisation and managing. I simply showed them that there is an alternative through the use of Simplexity Theory as practice and helped guide them through the transition.

132

Whilst there are on the face of things similarities in Lean Systems approach, these are incidental. The quest of my approach is freedom, fun, trust, happiness and fulfillment of the workers and not 'stripping of process waste' or gaining a systems analysis of each process. Allowing the passion of people to come to the fore results in Lean and Agile 'symptoms' (increasing productivity, reduction in waste) but again, in some it doesn't, it's not the purpose. The purpose is simply to demonstrate, if we engage people as human and subjective, we achieve many lean/agile results but in a way that's not defined to a fixed process or set of methodologies. It results also in quite significant improvements  in staff happiness ranging from, for example at BGCBC, less than 15% happy in their work prior to the intervention to over 89% post change.

### Other results include:
Do You Trust Management?
    Prior - 94% - No    Post 91% - Yes
Do you feel empowered in work?
    Prior 78% - No    Post 94% - Yes
Are you in a Trusted Workplace
    Prior 98% - No    Post 83% - Yes
Are you able to make suggestions in work to improve service/outputs?
    Prior 68% - No    Post 87% - Yes
Do you feel BGCBC appreciates the work you do?
    Prior 89% - No    Post 96% - Yes
Do you feel you have the 'tools' to do the job?
    Prior 63% - No    Post 82%- Yes
Are you delivering a 'Good Service' to the Public of BGCBC
    Prior 67% - No    Post 89% - Yes

Staff Response Rate - 92% (987 aver. return)

In the end the Council Leader Des Hillman was ousted by the incredibly silly games of the other less informed Councillors as part of the democracy and democratic games in BGCBC. The HRD Mark McIntyre also moved on and with the fear of change from the Welsh Assembly Government threatening mergers, change and reduced funding the council slowly reverted back to type. Traditional, hierarchical, power-seeking, non-risk public service through committee.

I was asked to 'leave' as they saw me as disruptive, but this was only the surface excuse. The problem was I was brought into help by the old CEO and now ousted Leader of the Council. Any successes attributed to these people could not be supported by the Councillors now in charge, so 'it': the work over the past two years had to 'go'.... And it did...me!

The work/impact is still there, and I am amazed that even today I can open my door to a Binman, Road Worker, Street Cleanser to HR Officer who seek advice or a place of refuge to moan and groan at 'how it is' and, 'how it could have been'...

# Chapter 11
# Specific interview findings

What I have here in this chapter are specific interview findings from various companies, public and private sectors: A narrative that will hopefully help you understand the real meaning of engagement and honest communication.

Some of the interview data listed here confirms the earlier discussion in this book that existing management practices must give way to more democratic and facilitative leadership if public sector, or private for that matter, improvement and modernisation are to work effectively and be sustainable for the longer term.

As one senior manager suggested, *'we fail to select activities – the matrix organisation needs re-evaluation and central functions such as Audit are costly and demotivating, adding no value to the client service.'* At this point all I was asking is do we need change! This is quite normal, in that people, most people are aware change is needed in order to survive and what I say these days about removing 'management' is quite well known.

From another simple question one suggested that, *'innovation comes from people and therefore people are the most important asset we have,'* and as the following series of quotes indicate, there is a critical need for a stronger emphasis on recognising that employees are integral to organisational performance within the complex systems.

Such as....*'I am here to learn, be treated with respect and to get the job done. Also, I am here to help where needed and discuss new ways to continue to make the organisation the great place that it should be. When you are not respected from the top then you cannot expect your colleagues to treat you with respect'* – this comment was from a long standing employee in Social Work.

Other common responses are:
- *'Too much stress on process reduces flexibility.'*
- *'Too much time is spent in convincing each other rather than working as a team by assigning clear goals, objectives and sharing responsibilities.'*
- *'Corporate objectives look good on paper, but how many of us actually follow and implement them?'*
- *'There are far too many targets, measures and Performance Indicators. We employ people to make these up and then monitor them in our services. By doing this we have removed the focus of the service itself, and now worry about making sure the target forms and procedures are done. Rubbish, if you ask me!'*

When I asked a team supervisor who was clearly, against giving up control, power and the next management goal of more management and that elusive career path stated: ***'The organisation is a top-down organisation. That structure might have been applicable during the years when we were small, but today we have more service demands and fire fighting processes. This type of organisation results in placing people in "silos" which hinders open*** *communication.   Sometimes working towards common goals, makes people fearful of taking a chance to recommend new ideas and approaches, and reduces the feeling of reward and accomplishment.'* She went on to say *'New ideas should be celebrated, not quashed. We could do a lot more, have a better quality product, and a happier work force by rethinking who we are and how we can allow our people to get there in the most efficient way.'*

Anyone who undertakes ethnography or deep 'in the jungle' type of research, quickly learns that the more you relax the more the research highlights key areas and perceived truths of those in the organisation with you. One Chinese worker stated about a week into the research, *'Managers need to get out of their offices and manage by walking around," and promote the corporate culture.'* And *'Information is in different places not centralised, and is duplicated hundreds of times by them to justify the existence.'* This is so unusual for so many reasons, firstly as a Chinese culture they rarely openly criticise the leadership like this, and secondly to open up to a westerner (big nose) even though they understood I wasn't going to report back.

The next few are from manufacturing in the UK and USA
*'We pay far too much attention to the top layers of management, and all they do is stop us working and doing what we know we can do.'*

*'Personally I think we are encouraged to work and we have support areas to help us. I do think there are too many managers and too many councillors whose behaviour is awful!'*

*' Having some helpful mates working together is also critical to success, let us get on with it, and it will work better.'*

*'I am not clear as to how our departmental goals meet the vision, but opportunities to interact with my counterparts are beginning to be more available.'*

**'We have too many management projects in parallel. Are we sure someone is co-ordinating them?'**

*'Communication culture is by far the most urgent topic to improve within a team & from upper management. Processes are not in place - tools do not exist. Corporate objectives are not clear to teams and updates are too irregular to make people feel that they are members of a community.'*

**'HR has to be more oriented to employees, especially at mid level.' Communication has to be improved between the different departments. We also need to be more informed about the civic centre and corporate strategies to be able to see the real goal.'**

*'More intensive integration could be good for the organisation and staff. It won't happen though because managers don't like giving up power to see improvements.'*

**'Here each person does his work without taking into account the ideas of the others. Here there are people who are always going to prosper by being above others. We are not a team.'**

*'Many managers are significantly booked up with administrative duties, reporting and formal meetings and don't*

have enough time to do their own management job. This creates an intermediate management layer where they delegate parts of their jobs.'

*'I just would like to highlight the fact that training to standard processes and procedures are not often adapted to people at various levels and that may be the reason why they are not always followed by all employees.'*

'I think it is necessary to check if all the people involved on the output of services have the competence and skills needed, which should improve the people competence and Skills "technical and managerial." This will be necessary to ensure a solid impact group for analysing and resolving all the problems we might have.'

*'I work in Admin and Finance. The amount of reporting has increased dramatically over the last year. We report on results over and over again with no end or point.'*

'In our particular part of the organization, the manager does not seem to trust any of his "subordinates". This has caused many issues between us and although we all trust each other and work well together, there is absolutely no trust in our immediate manager nor in his ability to bring the group as a whole, back together.'

*'In the last years, the environment has changed for the worst, due to more jobs than can be done out at same time - the top management are working in a panic, due to big losses in the services – they are not taking care of the roots of the problem.'*

'It is important to create mentorship for newcomers with some experienced people in the Company. This mentorship is not just an HR issue but should be internalised within each function'

**'HR has failed at every point. The managers here only think of themselves, hide the truth and fail to motivate anyone. We've missed the point of being here and that's to serve the customers. Managers and little Hitler's rule the place and even when we bring in consultants we fail to take on board their ideas, even though we all agreed to take it forward. Managers are worried about their positions and not our customers.'**

'My personal values are not shared by many of my co-workers as their objectives are often not in line with mine. We lack common goals across departments.'

**'Problems can only be solved through actions and face to face talking, and not through e-mails.'**

'The management (top level and below) only have their own personal targets in mind. They are not aware that behind each employee is a human being. They are focused on figures and are never interested in solving the "normal" people's problems. They only take care of themselves.'

**'Many problems arise in daily working, due to many interfaces and to many links to several bosses (I have five "bosses" I have to deal with).'**

'The pressure is so high, that many people get ill and/or are totally demotivated. The mood on our site is terrible.'

*'The changes are difficult to implement because people are resistant to change.'*

**'The demands, the customers and the technology are moving so fast that we have to react quickly to these changes if we want to be the best in the marketplace and not the worst.'**

*'There seems to be very little opportunity for personal advancement. Internal vacancies are seldom advertised, the post is usually filled by somebody selected according to some internal hidden agenda.'*

**'The organisation is complicated, which hinders quick and effective decision-making, and provision of too many reports and too much information.'**

*'The values of trust, teamwork and action need to be demonstrated by leaders in business when involving inter-business issues.'*

**'We have to be more customer centric in our way of working, through processes and in organisation. It's compulsory to be able to develop business and to be sure to deliver right products and services.'**

*'We spend too much time in reading e-mails and policies. This is effectively sapping valuable time. A method or process must be put in place so stop this waste.'*

**'Well, in my opinion no one cares about people, although that is very important nowadays, but being honest I do not feel that there is any care for employees.'**

# The Issues

The notion that any work environment is perfect is of course flawed. However in this case, as described in many facets above, the flaw is in the persistence of managerialism in Public Service provision. This counters the many messages proposed in many government White Papers, such as the 'The New Public Services, modern, dependable" (1997). In this publication rhetoric aimed to reframe Public Services thinking to modernist values, were to be discarded in favour of a moral focus, freedom of choice and self-management with the confines of the old ethos that the patient is 'king' and demand the 'control'. The Govt. proposed a shift from a mechanistic model of management towards a more fluid, organic and responsive system. The paper and Govt. now recognise the value of front line staff in the delivery of quality measures to Service and patient care. However, far from removing bureaucracy from the Public Services, these transformations have resulted in what is seen as the increased status of the 'professional manager' and a leadership style that remains autocratic and authoritarian. This is not the fault of the 'managers' themselves, something which I am at constant pains to point out in my talks and appearances at conference and on the radio (I avoid TV these days as I have a face for Radio). Managerialism is a product of the systems, traditional thinking, business education, business literature and NOT the people who do it.....management...! They simply act out what is expected, and desired by this thing called 'organisation'. Once these managers see an alternative, a place where leadership and people drive the outputs and top-line they are able to adapt.

Anyhow: The Western world's 'globalised thinking' and promises of economical gains and quality improvements through performance management, have been elusive and all evasive even today after the lesson in private sector demonstrate little or no results. The public sector vision however has not seen this reality and results have been contrary to expectation. In brief, the managerialism culture, has seen a reduction in co-operation and co-ordination, stifling co-evolutionary potential, and increasing the levels of stress in frontline staff and has had a tendency for centralised decision-making which is the opposite to the above Government thinking and White Papers.

These are symptoms about which anyone in the world of DNA and Simplexity would not be surprised: in effect the reduced ability of the front line staff to react and adapt to the dynamic needs of the service and 'customers'. What is more, existing staff feel threatened and any proposed motivational benefits for front-line staff have failed to materialise. The staff feel more undervalued than ever before. Indeed one member of staff in a public service provision stated *it's now all about the paper, than the people'* meaning simply that the service was bureaucratic, slow and not customer focussed, which was echoed throughout the 300 strong Adult Social Service department.

## The Power…. Oh the Trust

The problems stand with the significance of managerialism in the private sector, whilst still not in favour under any circumstances if honest, management of the public sector needs to be warned of the significance of the spread of such 'machine' perspectives and tools in the human service provision. There is no real quarrel with the notion of efficiency as such, but the key issue is that humans are not efficient- they can be effective, but never efficient. The inherent problem lies in the loss of social intelligence, the subjectivity of each human and with the number and range of conflicting discourses, which all add to the unique way each of us works.

Horton (2003) makes the crucial point that I quite like, although managerialism can provide more clarity over standards, objectives and expectations, its business-level ethos is in conflict with humans, human-mess and culture. Any concept of a 'public service ethos' may be somewhat abstract and difficult to quantify (ask any of my past MBA students whom I have tortured getting them to explain their organisations' vision, purpose and structures), but in recent times this has definitely been invaded by a more accountancy-based focus. It seems that this 'new' focus increases the expectation away from the social and emotional intelligence of the individuals towards the notion of central command, a brain, and control doctrine defined simplistically by management discourse.

In contrast to this view it is also suggesting that in, for example, Swedish Public Service systems, the business- like focus had created a heterogeneous, fluid, and human organisation. Yet in most of the organisations I have experienced in the past 15 years the diversity, and professional expertise of the people within has seen managerialism encroach, remove and damage the natural capacity of those within the service to lead it the way they see fit. The problem with Simplexity of the public provision is that it limits the usefulness of public sector managerialism. It stands in direct conflict if I'm honest and despite the work of

DNA I've failed miserably when I have attempted to compromise the notion of Simplexity and traditional management. The worth of management techniques currently adopted, aiming to simplify the complexity of a system is rather nebulous and on the face of it daft. The growth and continued growth, in the face of all its failings, of performance management, professional (meaning managers) development, traditional leadership and strategic planning all suggests that the alternative perspective of Simplexity thinking would confront, rather than reduce, the unpredictable dynamics of the human social system.

My work, as you've read, critically reflects on this thing called management and its emphasis on input and output, control and efficiency in the Public Services and public sector in general, but any organisation that has humans in it. The work I do challenges the view that the 'professional manager' will end the 'crisis' in the Public Services, indeed what we see and the evidence we gather, as detailed above, at each client organisation, indicated the complete opposite.

'Power and Authority' in roles and structures, made-up by the organisation seems to dominate the communication by staff with perceived more or less responsibility which leads to breakdowns in real information, trust and honesty. They are 'given' permission or are 'allowed' to convey certain information to other staff in the organisation. Referred to as 'orders' to others this authority or permissions seems to be perceived to exist 'way out of the reach' of many employees in the organisation. *"I think in some areas, you're only told and it's on a need to know basis" (01) another added "I think the chosen few are told what they're need to be told and then the rest of us are told what they would like us to be – the bit that they would like us to be known, you know, there are "I'll tell you that bit because..." (38).*

This perception of a hierarchy in communication flow based on 'authority' and 'need to know basis', is building a perceived 'pass-the-parcel' culture of communication between differing agents throughout the system. *"I think because it [communication] seems to go down the line rather than direct to Processing, it will go to Middle Management, then to someone else and then just goes through too many channels to get to the person it's aimed at." (41).* The data provides insight that communication within the areas is seen as good, constructive, and continuous with staff engaging in regular feedback and discussion within their respective teams. However, communication between staff across project divisions and between management and staff is not good. *"It's [communication] good within us lot and within the areas of the factory, once you're outside I don't think it's very good Management, I don't think it's very good at all." (41). One staff commented "Communication in the team is good at times, but far from perfect. I think it's good, you know, we can communicate with each area of the factory, it's no problem...but we don't trust people at all, especially the managers" (04)*Communication in locations is relatively good and at times informal between members of the system (sections and projects). However communication within Enterprise, especially from senior members of the system, is seen as extremely poor, untrusted, with incomplete and outdated information. Staff at a perceived lower level are not kept up to date, even when the information and/or decision has a professional and personal impact on them. *"I think we're*

146

*improving, as I said a moment ago, we're improving because we are now, we've set up an informal meet that goes back to each of the projects and its... we feeds back what we're talking about and what we're trying to achieve.... Nothing here is open or transparent.... its not working, terrible I know, but its not" (07)*

The formal provision of incomplete and outdated information, coupled with a culture of authority and hierarchy in communication flow is propagating informal network following an organic culture of 'Chinese whispers'. Staff perceptions that they are not getting the 'entire picture' or 'full information', that members of the system who have perceived power and decision making authority are not being open with them, resort to reliance on informal networks for communication. One staff commented that the enterprise was *"Very, very secretive. Very secretive, indeed. You get some Managers come up and they're like talking in the corridors, and like whispering and things like that and you're just like hmmm, okay, what's going on there then?, and you'd ask like the managers and they would go by your Team Leaders whispering while you're at your desk, where they should be going to another room to discuss things." (02)*

Communication within teams/sections within commands appears to occur through natural face to face modes of communication (e.g., we just go to talk to them). This is a far more informal means of communication that occurs naturally and organically within the system. Changes to physical properties within the office has/can influence perceived connectivity and interaction between team/section members (e.g., bringing team leaders onto the section). Staff perceptions of increased connectivity and interaction within and between fellow staff in team/section in commands appears to dilute the need for more formal communication.

Communication between management and frontline project and decision making staff (within locations) is perceived to be

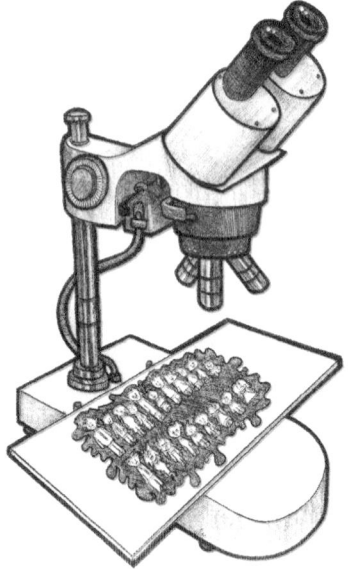

inherently one-way and dominated by feedback to staff especially on performance (i.e. targets) and frequent changes to processes (decided by management). For example, weekly manager feedback (one-way) and the issuing of bulletins 'by checking regime' about change on decisions/processing benefits with little consideration of the impact of that bulletin or guidelines for implementation (or further consultation).

What strongly resonates is the perception that management try to communicate, but that an underlying 'uncertainty' or 'fear' exists, that they are scared or draw away from receiving feedback from staff, distancing themselves, due to the advancing years and experience of those performing the roles and that the expectation is that they 'have' to have the answers. *"I just feel sometimes that we have got a check list regime in this factory and a section that checks work and they do a lot of that, yet crap still goes out to customers, I know, but sometimes what will happen, they'll issue instructions and we'll perhaps get something out that something has changed and literally they'll just issue like the bulletin about it, with no, sort of, guidance or anything ...." (05)*

Trust is imperative as a foundation to share knowledge and experiences and requires open, honest communication to thrive, human social bonds to have been developed. Perceptions evident within the system note clusters of trust to exist within the organisation, especially within frontline teams (i.e., commands and sections). However, limited perceptions of trust occur between agents, they are perceived to reside in more senior roles and those that reside on role on the frontline – processing and decision making staff within teams and between locations. One employee stated *"you never know what's held back, if you know what I mean?  If they're [management] holding anything back, do you know, because the Managers know more than us".* Another employee stated *"For the last couple of years there's been, like, these office closures or moves and things like that, so none of us knows exactly what's going on, I suppose.  So I just think that the Management, I think they know more what's going on more than they're letting on, if you know what I mean?" (02)*

Agents co-exist in a culture of increasing performance checking and evaluations through management imposed targets and metrics. A perceived suffocation is evident and limited autonomy, with agents in the system not having the freedom to grow and  develop, with a constant culture of distrust and performance- checking through unnatural performance metrics (i.e., targets), called 'expectations' (not targets). 'Being Watched', 'management over them', 'having to

149

do what we are told to do'. However, it was noted in the transcripts that senior management have/are trying to change this, move towards more quality than quantity focus, although this message is not always consistent.

Within the system there appears a genuine mistrust of 'what management' are doing' and that there is a bigger picture that most are not aware of and that management are not telling staff everything. Senior staff working on projects which are secret seems to fuel rumours of a culture of 'smoke and mirrors' and distrust. One long term employee commented *"trust? Yeah, do, sort of, we if we trust them [management] [laughs]? They always seem to be up to something. Well, we always think they are. They could spend all day having a meeting about something and they take about, you know, ten minutes to tell you about it [laughs] and stuff like that, which – and I have never been to their meetings, so don't really know, but they just give you the impression sometimes that there's more going on than they tell you [laughs]." (03)*

When individuals with whom we are interconnected, especially significant people in our lives listen, value our contribution and reward us appropriately, we feel valued. This directly impacts on our sense of self-worth and self-esteem, creating a positive self-image allowing us to work to our full potential. Evident in the research were perceptions of feeling disrespected by both? management. Perceptions of 'being a number', treated as a 'commodity' were evident in the transcripts. For example, individuals 'acting up' from one role to another due to staff shortages and workload demands shared feelings of 'being used' and 'unappreciated' for doing more. In essence during times when the organisation needs you and when they don't, you are "plonked" back down, down in role, status and remuneration. Another example resonates

150

in the constant 'move changes' without consultation or perceived thought as to the consequences and personal effects of those moves on an individual.

A main form of change that seems to occur is relative to room and desk changes to additional manager layers. These changes seem to occur often and without adequate consultation with the agents within the system on whom they have a direct effect. This change is therefore disruptive to the organic and natural interconnectivity that occurs and has developed throughout the teams. As the teams develop, a natural and organic system of interaction and interdependency occurs, but/ so when an unnatural system structure [perceived by management] is imposed, disruption occurs. This has a significant impact on performance and agent satisfaction within the system. In addition, there is a perception of always trying or doing something new. On the one hand this was perceived as quite favourable, in that the system is constantly evolving, however on the other it was perceived as negative in that as soon as agents have gained the knowledge and understanding necessary for something, it changes. This is highlighted by one employee *"we've done things in the past and, like, you try them and maybe they work, maybe they don't and you only end up doing it for maybe a couple of years and then they come up with something else to try doing, so, you know.. They always seem to be trying something different [laughs]." (03)* Another continues *"the best part of the few years I've been in, there's constant changes. There's changes all the time. And they can become a little bit stressful at times, but I think all in all, I think most people who work within the office cope with changes quite readily. And changes aren't always a bad thing." (36)*

# Award Winning Results – Leadership from Within

## DNA definitive case study

What you are about to read are just a sample of the changes we have completed in company. This is not to brag or illicit new business, but to simply show what can be achieved with true engagement, leadership and trust. The client in the first case is Ministry of Justice Department: National Offender Management Service (NOMS) Contact Centre: Timescale: Sept 2013 - May 2014. The second Monmouthshire County Council Department: Children and Youth Offending Services Timescale: February 2014 - August 2014. And lastly, Cornwall Council Department: Community and Support Service (CaSS) Timescale: June 2013 - September 2013 (Update and revisit in March 2014).

*Key Issue Could **Team Empowerment** in an Service Level Agreed (SLA) driven environment aid higher performance and morale?*

*We started working at the MoJ DNA with the Contact Centre teams after quite a lengthy and difficult contract debate, taking me over a year, with 19 presentations and mixed interviews/meetings, so the notion of starting this in September 2013 filled me with relief and a little excitement even before I got to speak to frontline staff. I was also a little nervous if honest, given the hoops jumped and the standards require when onsite, from dress code, security checks to the sheer volume of work the Contact Services dealt with on a daily basis. I was also starting this with a new team, including 4 new pre-intervention research team and this would be the first full-change DNA programme for Steve Eaton MBE and Co-Director Andy McCann. Not that I was worried about the last two, only could be all be in the same place together without mass chaos and conflict. Can you imagine us three in the same room...haha!*

The Ministry of Justice just in case you don't know, operated a dedicated service centre from offices in South Wales. Three service driven departments exist at the location, working alongside each other, supplying vital support for the needs of a 1200 strong workforce based over 4 locations. Services include HR, Finance Advice, Payroll Support and Legal. These were over 3 floors and we started in the middle floor, Contact Services, who were directly in contact (excuse the obvious) with customers. So we were in the right place.

With varying degrees of Service Level Agreements (SLA) in place, from answering calls in 32 seconds, to replying to emails in 5 days, to Voice of the Customer (VOC) satisfaction scores, the need for continual information sharing throughout the entire division, increasing volumes and types of services offered, each department faces its own challenges when it comes to compliance, efficiency and staff morale.

I have to say from the outset, he Ministry of Justice is dedicated to continual service delivery improvement and efficient customer response at all times. The level of professionalism was also incredibly high from bottom to top in the organisation, which was personified by Laurence

154

Thomas, Daniel Davies and Ireen Lock. I mention these three in particular as there were many, but these three senior managers, simply got it...rare breed. Laurence who was the instigator two years ago, heard me talk at a roundtable event and we plotted the downfall of management ever since this moment. I have to say his intellect, was matched only by his ability in foreign languages and love for human beings. The sad thing was that by the time we started this project, Laurence had decided to take early retirement and never got to see the fruits of his initial hard work and resilience in getting me and DNA to the MoJ table.

The MoJ had guidelines for each department that were clear, and customer service satisfaction placed at the heart of all targets and expectations. As a progressive employer the MoJ contracted DNA Definitive to look at areas where management and delivery improvements could be made, whilst empowering staff and increasing employee job satisfaction. But only on the second floor with the Contact Service Teams.

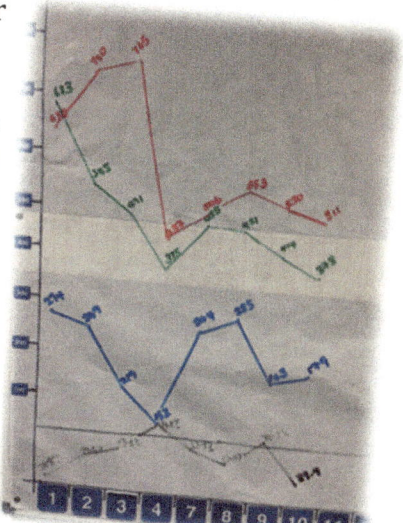

Caroline, a Service Area Manager for example headed up the contact centre for the NOMS division for three years, with a total of 6 years working for the Ministry of Justice. Her team of 100 staff respond to the daily needs of the prison services employees across the UK. The setting of tasks and targets has always been clearly identified for the team and were continually referred to when assessing division success and customer satisfaction levels.

Targets for the team included:
- Approximately 200 pieces of work to be completed by each team member each day
- 3 day Service Level Agreement (SLA) in place - each customer query (email or telephone) to be responded to and dealt with within 3 working days
- Customer Surveys are sent out each week - Customer Satisfaction Score target set at 80%
- Calls to be answered within 2 mins and a 90% achievement record each month
- Work in Progress (WiP) list to be reduced in size, considerably - continually at over 200 backlog queries to be dealt with on an ongoing basis

The reality was that although staff were all performing well and with speed, the Work in Progress list wasn't being dealt with fast enough due to the volume of new queries coming in on a daily basis, staff were being regularly asked to work overtime to deal with the backlog, increasing costs, and customer satisfaction surveys revealed that scores continually came in between 70-80%, below the target. In addition staff morale was low, and without the incentive options of a commercial contact centre environment, it was becoming increasingly difficult for Caroline to motivate and inspire her team.

**The Solution**

DNA Definitive met with Caroline and her team and discussed the challenges they were facing, together and as individuals. They encouraged input and feedback on a group basis, and also held separate sessions with each team member over a period of two weeks. As part of these sessions they discussed things like removing targets, WIP posters, moving more experienced staff to sit by less experienced staff, having a floor walker to instantly deal with problems from customers etc. The biggest issue was, however, stopping Team Leaders from producing daily and hourly statistics on each member's performance.

Caroline said: "I have to be honest and say I was skeptical about the proposed changes at first. My team was already under pressure to deliver in the time they had available, and they kept being asked to engage with DNA and spent many hours talking with them and receiving coaching."

Andy McCann, DNA Definitive, explained: "Working within such a progressive and customer focused organisation like the MOJ Shared Services Contact Centre is always a privilege. The challenge is always to identify and affirm the existing good practice, while also promoting a search as to whether people, systems and processes could be benefit the customer even more. We have found that one effective way of doing this is through our guest speaker Performance Insights Programme, where we bring in individuals from other, unrelated, environments and professions to talk through their challenges, their focus and how they measure success. In this way, the questions raised come from within - as do many of the answers!"

Indeed, following a visit and presentation by DNA Definitive's sponsored x2 World & European Sailing Champion, Sam Brearey, staff member Hannah Ottery (NOMS HRCC) said, "This was a brilliant insight, and Sam's definition of a high performing team really challenged me and my team in our work."

In 2 weeks the team began to make some of their own decisions about the best way to approach the challenges they were facing. They began to question everything and asked themselves what they were doing, why they were doing it and what they could do to change it. The staff began to feel empowered and as if they really could effect changes that would make a significant and sustainable difference.

As the division of experience across the team was often unevenly stretched and training less experienced staff had become difficult to fit into the working day, the team came up with the idea of a 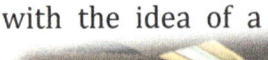 daily floor walker. This meant that at any one time there was an experienced person available to support the more junior members throughout the day, and could respond to queries on the fly as needed.

**The Impact**

In addition to a happier, more empowered workforce the number results also speak volumes:
- for the first time the 3 day SLA target is being met regularly, in some cases volumes of queries are answered within 1-2 working days
- the Work in Progress list of outstanding queries has been reduced by 80%

- Customer Satisfaction Scores (from the weekly surveys) are now consistently 90% and above
- A significant increase in calls are being dealt with at first resolution level (with Floor Walker assistance support)
- No overtime has been worked since 1st November 2013.
- The staff are happier and more fulfilled

# DNA definitive case study

**Client:**

***Title: DNA Definitive support Children's Services through a period of refocusing and relocation***
*DNA works with 100-strong team to support 'children first' policy alongside compliance and consistency*

## The Background

Monmouthshire County Council Children's Services provides a multi-disciplinary service offering health and social care disciplines via a team of 100 people. Professionals include social workers, contact officers, youth offending officers, administrators, fostering services, and more.

In 2013 a restructure of the service took place within the Children's Services aspect of the department and in 2014 the majority of the team moved from two locations to one location at the Council offices in Magor.

## The Challenges

*"The very nature of working with children means that you have to carefully balance the needs of the client (which is at the heart of everything we do) alongside good practice and compliance."*
Tracy Jelfs,
Head of Children's Services, Monmouthsire County Council

A team that was recovering from a restructure, which in some cases resulted in members hiding behind policies and procedures and avoiding levels of responsibility, meant that

160

there was a general reluctance to embrace change and reassess existing procedures, systems and to think about their working practices differently.

Issues with IT, the amount of casework across the department and often over complicated procedures created barriers to delivering services that ensured the most efficient and effective outcomes.

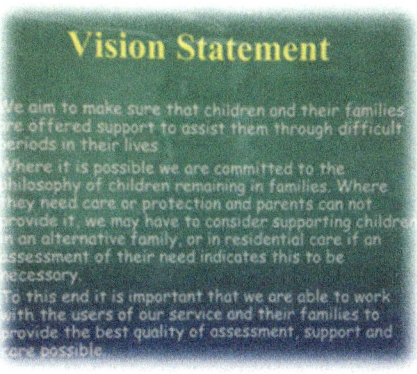

*"We wanted to encourage social workers to 'play and engage' again and to be focused completely on where they could best meet the needs of the children and families, not be bogged down with systems and hierarchies. We wanted staff to become leaders and move away from the micro-management of teams, ultimately with the aim of improving practice as well as motivation amongst staff."*

## The Solution

DNA Definitive met with Tracy and many members of the entire service team. Staff were given the choice of speaking with DNA or not, and the sessions varied in length.

Questions were asked such as - *"What would need to change to make it fun and enjoyable for you to come to work?"*

Working alongside Tracy, Paul identified areas where it was felt change was necessary and in many cases Tracy already had potential solutions in mind, but needed the independent and impartial support to instigate those changes.

The team structure charts were discarded in an effort to truly breakdown institutional barriers and improve practice and maturity across the board. A flatter structure meant that every team member had access to every other team member, without having to go through a hierarchy of contact and management.

Staff were discouraged from micro-managing teams, and to demonstrate her own commitment to change, Tracy decided not to respond to emails that weren't directly sent to her (i.e. not just CC'ed in) for a period of two weeks.

*"As with any senior staff member, there are emails and information where you're copied in just as a fail-safe mechanism. I wanted to move away from that to encourage staff, who are extremely capable, to make the decisions themselves, and to come to me when they genuinely deemed it necessary and had exhausted their own skills and knowledge. This wasn't to avoid decision-making on my part, but to*  *empower the workforce and encourage responsibility. I am always available for any staff member, but spreading both the skills and responsibility is vital for the sustainability of the team and also individual career progression."*

As a result of only reading emails directly addressed to her, alongside a strategy of prioritization of all tasks and a focus on reducing meetings that were duplication or not aligned to the focus of the work Tracy cleared four extra days in her diary in the first month.

Simple solutions such as securing mobile phones for staff members who were out on the road and sometimes in difficult and challenging situations, was something that DNA also worked with the team to secure. Establishing a weekly work plan meeting and establishing a Service dedicated web page on the intranet has also worked towards improving internal communications and raising the profile of the good work the Service provides.

**The Impact**

The department is still in a state of change and internal reassessment, but the building blocks of greater and wider responsibility and motivation have been established.

*"We had previously worked with other methodologies, which focused on the idea that if you sort out the systems then the rest will follow and work as a result. I instinctively didn't buy into this practice and with people, specifically children, as our key focus, we had to ensure we were thinking in more 'human' terms and the ultimate unpredictability and chaos that accompanies this, along with changes to working cultures that were required.*

*We need our staff to be able to make decisions and take responsibility in what can often be quite challenging circumstances. Systems and procedures have a place in this but they are not the key and will not provide the ultimate answer.*

*Dr. Paul Thomas and the DNA Definitive team have encouraged and supported both myself and the staff to take a leap of faith in many circumstances, whilst absolutely capitalizing on the talent and expertise of the team.*

*The improvements in technology, internal communications and a flatter structure have gone a long way to improving vital communications and ensuring all staff have a wider knowledge of the successes and challenges of the Service as a whole."*

# DNA  definitive case study

Client:

## Title: Improving frontline engagement and communication – catalyst for change

*DNA definitive works with Cornwall Council Community and Support Service (CaSS) team to improve communication and engagement between senior management and frontline workers*

## The Background

CaSS employs 300 staff across a number of divisions and locations, from social workers to voluntary Careers and drivers.  Safeguarding and high-level service delivery is at the heart of CaSS engagement with clients, and a continually changing market place presents consistent challenges.

A series of HR based surgeries with members of staff to gauge feedback, concerns and challenges highlighted some staff issues surrounding morale, lack of qualitative communication and future plans for the team. The decision was made to outsource the next stage of engagement with staff to enable an independent and impartial review, and to challenge current internal practices.

DNA Definitive was selected from knowledge of previous work carried out with Local Authorities, and for their passionate commitment to working with frontline staff.

## The Challenges

Communication between senior leaders and frontline staff and overall engagement was identified as requiring significant improvement. Staff morale was low with concerns about the future felt by many. There was a heavy reliance on processes and administration, which many felt was placing heavier emphasis on paperwork and procedures than on the individuals who use the services and indeed staff members themselves.

Staff felt decisions were made without a democratic approach and there was a lack of consultation, discussion or debate with the people delivering services at the frontline.

**The Solution**

DNA Definitive interviewed a large cross-section of the 300 strong team, as well as external stakeholders, other division members and some CaSS team family members. The focus was on unearthing the concerns and challenges across the board, but particularly the staff delivering services to the public.

The Senior Team was faced with feedback, often negative, about processes, procedures and attitudes, with a lack of trust at the forefront and for a month some processes, such as appraisal systems and other administrative management led activities were suspended.

The DNA Definitive approach is based on chaos first followed by autonomous solutions. A degree of turbulence was experienced across the entire division, as the issues and real challenges were unearthed, expressed and shared. There was some suspicion, worry and concern at the outset of the process as staff were introduced to the methods and opportunities for engagement.

Creating an environment where feedback, input and communication from all levels was encouraged and expected, frontline staff were then challenged with devising new solutions and procedures moving forward, to alleviate objections and concerns about efficiencies and service delivery focus.

Connectivity and interdependence between divisions and individuals was recognised as vital for the service, to re-energise the team and improve service delivery and safeguarding.

**The Impact**

DNA Definitive is viewed as the catalysts for a period of change at CaSS, with sustainable benefits for the Service. Communication has improved, particularly between the Senior Leadership Team and Team Leaders. Team Leaders are invited on rotation to meetings and a monthly extended leadership team meeting is also now happening with minutes circulated to the Team Leader Group. Regular bulletins are now also circulated to the service as a whole to keep teams up to date.

Increased face-to-face communication is happening and has helped people to re-connect and build high levels of trust. There is less of a void felt between the senior team and the service and staff feel they now have the environment and opportunities to challenge and contribute to decisions. This in turn as reduced the need to use electronic communication helping the Leadership Team to spend more time with frontline staff and Service Users.

Corporate Resources are used more efficiently and some systems and processes have been developed and amended to provide more responsive support to staff. A simplified internal performance management system has been introduced. Staff training and recruitment has been reviewed which has contributed to the development of shared values across the service, which was a key element of the project objectives.

The input from DNA has brought new focus to the team and instigated an environment that encourages and supports improved communication, discussion and staff engagement, whilst also placing expectations on all staff, at all levels to identify opportunities for ongoing change and improvement.

In an update meeting (March 2014, some 6 months on) the Senior Leadership Team were again realizing the key benefits of a more engaged workforce with clearer purpose and values of the service. Whilst there was still some turbulence in the system the staff felt much more confident and positive in the longer term future of the service and its position to help Adults.

One small aside story which seems small but is significant was the comment by one area manager, that only last week 'the staff in one centre asked if he would join their five-aside team, demonstrating significant improvements in trust and connectivity with all levels'.

# Chapter 12
# A Personal View

Rachel neither had business nor childcare experience when she had the idea to open her own day nursery, and she also knew that she only wanted to work during term time. With this criteria, the food quality manager and mother of two understandably had difficulty in persuading the bank manager to lend her the necessary finance.

But Rachel quickly found out that her lack of business knowledge and experience became the greatest asset of her new business. Indeed Rachel found that she could do business differently as with no 'formal' training or pre-existing ideas on what or how organisations 'should be' she could do it differently, in a 'non-conformist' way. The one thing she did understand was what it was like to be a working mum with children in day-care. Rachel realised that this was the logical place to start.

The business was set up in reverse, rather than stating *'This is the childcare we provide, do you want it?'* it was a question of, *'Tell us what childcare you want and we'll do our best to provide it.'* The focus of Rachel's new business was simply to ensure that customer needs were served. This included parents and children, with her staff a close second.

There was never any doubt that the provision would be anything less than the best available. Staff quickly learned that the reason they were there was to be the best and to have the answer to any question there might be and to ask; *'How would it be done in the best day nursery?'*

Rachel knew that the best day nursery needed to have the best staff, especially as Rachel had no intention of being there full time to control, monitor and 'police' her staff. The business goal was to employ confident and responsible decision makers who used their initiative and creativity and worked as a team to be good role models for the children whilst providing the very best care. Even before the legal requirements all staff were childcare qualified, although it soon became apparent that their certificates didn't cover the soft skills; primarily confidence. Rachel had no childcare qualifications and believed that those who did should be the ones making the decisions in the business. Why on earth should she be making decisions about the children when she employed experts who could do a much better job?

However, Rachel discovered that although the staff had the qualifications, information and, indeed, knew the answers to what they should do, they lacked the confidence to take action. The nursery was full of nursery nurses, phenomenal in their child caring skills, but totally unable to look parents in the eye or to lock out unexpected visitors while they gained authorisation – for fear of hurting their feelings.

A comprehensive training and support mechanism evolved which began with the nursery nurses being asked to describe the qualities of the best nursery nurses. They came up with 14 that were later labelled the 'Star qualities'.

- Supportive of each other
- Confidence
- Rapport Builder
- Consistent Reliable
- Open & Honest
- Responds well to change
- Responsible
- Enthusiastic
- Positive Attitude
- Communicator Teamworker
- Respects Confidentiality
- Initiative
- Decision Maker
- Works well under pressure

The business only wanted to employ people who had these 'Star qualities'. That meant encouraging those that were already employed to develop any of the 'star qualities' in which they were deficient. It also meant specifically looking for those qualities during recruitment. The company set about changing all aspects of the way they managed people, instigating a training programme to develop qualities in existing staff, a review and reward process to maintain 'star qualities' from day to day, and tailoring of the recruitment process to identify 'star qualities' in applicants for jobs.

Those who were already employed were encouraged through coaching and training to develop their fourteen 'star qualities'. Coaching very soon became the main action for each nursery manager.  Once the expectations of the team were raised and they understood and bought into the 'why?' manner of questioning what was being done, the manager was able to pass on many of her responsibilities.

When shift and staff/child ratios were handed over to the team – they decided amongst themselves who, what, where and when – not surprisingly, as they took control, their performance improved. Their input meant that they were working to suit themselves covering holidays, days off and realising that phoning in sick meant that it was the rest of the team's responsibility to find cover rather than their absence being the 'manager's problem'. Eventually it became the individual's responsibility to find cover.  All the staff were given the contact details of the authorised relief staff and were expected to have found a replacement before they phoned in. Unauthorised absences were reduced to a minimum and the team manager was able to use her time to continue coaching and get on with what she was best at.

Coaching took place both formally and informally. Formal reviews took place every six months when each individual was able to share how they felt they were demonstrating the 'star qualities,' in a one-to-one off site meeting with the team manager. Also available was their team's opinion as to how they shone as a star.  This took the form of a checklist with specific examples of an individual's performance that they could be congratulated for – highlighted by their colleagues.

Rachel made sure that focus was always on strengths and natural abilities. She recalls:

"We never saw the point of pouring negative energy onto what they were not doing. We found that by concentrating on personal successes, congratulating them, allowing everyone to enjoy the feeling of that success, self-confidence grew and the gaps got filled on their own. Taking on a new challenge from a position of confidence when you have just been praised in one area raised the likelihood of success in a new area. So it was OK to dare and risk – it was ok to make mistakes, there would be no punishment, it was a process that allowed everyone to learn about themselves and to learn how they might lean on each other. This was a process that allowed each of them to take it in turn to excel at what they were best at; everyone could accept that it was unlikely that any one person could be the best at everything. Rachel commented....

"As the team came to rely more and more on each other, absenteeism and sickness levels dropped and staff turnover was negligible – if ever the management team had to resort to the disciplinary procedure then they knew that they had failed as managers. The essence of the success of the child day care centre was that everyone knew their value within the team and therefore to the business. When confidence increased, all the staff addressed each other and received feedback knowing that their contribution was valued. Knowing the level of responsibility that was expected of them and that they could lean on the team to share in that responsibility, if disciplinary action was necessary it was obvious that they didn't get the company philosophy, that they had no idea of their value and the effect of their actions on the whole. We were all links in a chain, each were made up of different elements and however much some thought of themselves as key links in the chain, at the end of the day we were only as strong as the weakest link." She continued...

*"Building confidence was the foundation of our success; we found that soft skills could be achieved if we concentrated on finding ways to stretch everyone's comfort zones either through day-to-day challenges or through training days.*

What is particularly interesting is that the comfort zone of 'doing things well' was never really accepted. Rachel and her staff constantly looked to challenge and raise expectations without being 'explicit' or forced. This is again were a lot of Simplexity Leaders make small mistakes. Writing down Values or a Mission Statement almost destroys what exactly it is you are trying to 'do' as the daily routine. One they quickly become dated, and two they need to be lived, not written into a smart text, or sentence to enforce.

*"Day to day challenges could be anything from having to make a difficult call to a customer to presenting at a local school. When someone was experiencing a new situation they were assigned a 'comfort blanket'. 'Comfort blanket' was the term given to any person who could coach the team member in the challenging area, in whom they could confide their fears. Someone who would stand in the background ready to step in if required and who would be able to provide positive feedback and confirm that indeed the comfort zone walls had been breached! Comfort blankets weren't necessarily senior staff, it was any team member who had been there, done that – the team worked together using their individual strengths to help each other become the best nursery nurses.*

The greatest impact for me looking at Rachel's company was the element of fun, even when the work or training was serious, fun was never far behind:

*"More formal internal training took place at monthly meetings. Held out of hours, everyone gave their time for a one-hour evening meeting. Out of respect for everyone's effort the one-hour rule was always strictly adhered to and the agenda calculated to the minute so that no time was wasted and everyone would get away on time. Once again the aim was to have fun as we reaffirmed the fourteen star qualities in each other through games and activities and discussed topics which were generally sourced by external visits, parent suggestions or team ideas which had been gathered at ten minute weekly meetings.*

*"Ten minute weekly meetings were held by staff who worked in the same area. These had been quickly put in place when we realised that although everyone was working in a close environment and chatting to each other all day long – actually no one was really communicating! It was originally left to the team to decide the agenda, but the meetings were reduced to even more chat so eventually a brief structure was put in place. Six questions had to be asked, and to avoid 'Chinese Whispers' written records were kept; hits and misses of the previous week – something that should have got done this week but that we didn't get around to – planning the future week – noting children and parent queries – noting any gaps in training under the, 'I wish someone had told me ...' and Health and Safety issues.*

From time to time these turned into a list of complaints which were sent 'upstairs', to the office and Rachel. Whenever this happened the Team Leader coached the team listening to groans and encouraging the team to find their own answers. Occasionally, the Team Leader would forget herself and have fixed the problem in moments to everyone's satisfaction. The problem with this was simply the 'parent and child' relationship was established and then had to be unlearnt over the next few days. They learnt the hard way that this was a short-term solution as the team glimpsed a 'safe, soft' world with no responsibility – one where all the thinking was done for them and they could all moan when it went wrong. Then with all the effort of the previous months temporarily disregarded, it would be hard work getting back on track.

Frequently Rachel felt it would be quicker if she did things herself (and she was possibly right). Working as a team means that you go at the pace of the slowest which is frustrating, but two points prevailed, she didn't want to be there full time, so had to 'delegate' and she was trusting her business to 'the team' in her absence, so it was vital that boundaries and values were lived, set and breathed at all times. At times she felt that her biggest challenge – letting go and taking the risk of someone else doing it – was made harder by knowing that she could have done it better, or perhaps in accepting that that accolade wouldn't always belong to her and that there were others in the team who excelled where she didn't. Rachel found that by increasing her own confidence along with everyone else she too could commit to the, 'How would it be done in the best nursery?' and thus stay on track.

Rachel also found that getting everyone back on track and ensuring that they stayed on track was easier with outside help. External training involved either bringing in visitors or formal trainers. However, these were generally unconventional trainers who didn't rely on training plans or measures that did not address Rachel's aim of developing 'the fourteen? soft skills'.

So visitors were encouraged from all walks of life – anyone who would enhance the routine of the day and stimulate creativity in the team, from supermarket fruit and vegetable reps to mounted police on their horses.

Rachel continues: *"Two Saturdays a year, everyone gave up their time to attend training days hosted by trainers. The first rule was to ensure everyone had fun so that giving up a Saturday was worthwhile. A series of 'challenges' would be presented allowing the staff to confront their comfort boundaries again. No one could ever predict who in the company would excel in each area but through challenges that included driving 4x4s, walking on broken glass with trust falls, mud assault courses, breaking through planks of wood with our hands, we learned a lot about ourselves and each other and brought an increased confidence and self awareness back into work on the Monday morning.*

She continued *"Off-site visits were encouraged although difficult to maintain with the strict child/ staff ratios that we maintained. We loved visiting not only other providers but all workplaces who invested in their people, networking, and being inspired by quality employers and how they managed their staff whilst building relationships that opened up a whole world of expertise that was just a phone call away. During visits, the team never failed to be surprised at just how good they were, some part of them always bought into the 'only a nursery nurse' expectation of society. Enabling them to compare themselves favourably with traditionally more respected occupations was an overwhelming advantage and confidence boost."*

Congratulating success was considered essential – the business marketed the success of their philosophy and as a result won several business awards for their innovative approach to people management. Staff always attended the lavish award ceremonies that the company paid for, in favour of a traditional Christmas night out which the staff used to organise and pay for themselves.

To ensure the momentum of congratulating success was maintained, staff were encouraged to display the 14 'star qualities' to each other with a star of the month competition. Members of the team could award a WOW to anyone who they thought had demonstrated a 'star quality'. In giving a WOW, the team member had 'Walked on Water', and they were counted up at the end of the month and a bouquet of flowers presented to the person with the most 'WOW's at the monthly meeting. The photo of the winner was displayed prominently in the entrance for the children and parents to see. The newsletter involved parents in the scheme and a WOW from a parent soon became a coveted accolade.

As the business grew it became essential to employ new staff. Originally a traditional recruitment process of interviews by senior staff and trial days was used but this was found to be too time consuming, costly and unreliable, especially when the Team Leaders liked the applicant but the team did not. As the team began to develop their own 'star qualities', they became more and more demanding about new recruits and it became obvious that recruitment too would have to become team led. The responsibility for recruitment was therefore given to the team. Staff gave up their own time in the evenings to host events that were given a tight and strict timetable, thus acknowledging and respecting everyone's commitment.

Recruitment involved the whole team-observing candidates at role-play. This might be building 'Lego' bridges or spaghetti towers. They would watch interviewees interact with each other and chat to the applicants informally as well as asking them work-based questions, listen to their opinions on likely workplace scenarios and make a checklist of the demonstrated star qualities. It was again ...fun!

Rachel says, *"This served the business in more than one way – not only had we found an effective and more reliable recruitment process, but word about our business and how different we were spread, giving us a higher profile as an employer and childcare provider."*.

Originally the team experienced fear and were intimidated at the thought of employing someone, 'better than me'. Rachel had to learn to let go of employing the people she thought would be best and trust the team to choose who they would like to work with. As time passed and their confidence grew, everyone was more able to focus on the, 'Why are we here?' They only chose the very best candidates – because they worked at the very best nursery. Very soon, the team were completely responsible for employing new members and management were responsible only for the security and qualification checks, together with the references that were required to be verified by the Childcare Standards.

Of course, there were times when less than the full complement of staff turned up at recruitment nights. Then the responsibility was left to a few, although those who hadn't attended soon realised that they did not have as much of a voice when it came to reviewing the successful applicants during their probation because they had not been there to choose them in the first place. Staff also began to take the process for granted; the majority had not worked elsewhere and were oblivious of the important responsibility they had been given or the level of trust that had developed between the entire staff. They didn't appreciate what a big deal it was.

Interestingly, the process was not used for the promotion of Team Leaders. Loyalty and length of service was valued, based on the perceived fact that those loyal and long serving employees best knew the paradigm of the business. After many years it was noted that those recruited successfully by the team, were the first to leave when an 'original' Team Leader was put in charge to cover maternity leave. In the absence of senior staff member support, the team leader made herself a 'manager' and resorted to the old command and control tactics instead of trusting and encouraging responsibility in others.

Suddenly they were being managed by someone who was telling them what they could and couldn't do rather than allowing them to sort themselves out, as had been the experience for the previous five years. Suddenly they weren't being trusted anymore and four left within five months ... ouch! Interestingly, they all went on to at least supervisory positions in other nurseries.

# Chapter 13
# The Beginning not the End

### ... too much still to achieve

My research, experience and reading in China back in the late 90's quickly began to suggest to me that we are shaped by forces that are beyond our control and that cannot be harnessed, I suppose the external 'system'. I began to see that my own beliefs, which had given me such certainty and comfort, promoting the idea that if you keep to the rules and trust in superior power all will be well, were false and at times, looking back, complete nonsense. I even began to doubt that the management and organisational theory I had learned and applied reflected reality.

As a result of these doubts, I began, as you have read, to question my own understanding of management in organisations and, indeed, my own role as a manager, and have continued ever since, to the annoyance of most (sorry) as an academic. I realised that the theory I had learned did not truly reflect my experiences, but I was unable to express this freely for fear of being seen as different or, worse still, as not being 'management material'. Later this turned into a neat asset as an academic given the 'criticality' of the role, but it still didn't endear people to me. The manager is the product of traditional business structures and discourse taught in most business schools and lauded in all the big organisations as the way of doing business, that aim to facilitate centralised management control and adherence to formalised operational

181

processes. Indeed, we still see today that if there is a crisis it's because this thing called management has not controlled or bullied enough in the right places.

Managers are expected to use their status and position to justify their right to manage, through command and control, and are motivated to maintain the status quo.

## Competitive Advantage

Yet in my research over the past 15 years there are significant individual and organisational advantages to those who can adapt the fastest to emerging trends, trends we see as experience and instinct mixed together, while maintaining high performance in the short term. Simplexity has an incredible potential for delivering these outcomes as these 'leaders' are on the ground, listening, mixing, and influencing behaviours and vice-versa.

The 21st Century, Simplexity organisation allows the leader the capacity to improve both performance and future sustainability as they change accordingly to make the organizational output, not input in simply not spending time on rules, regulations, procedures, policies, etc. which all distract energy away from change and outputs. Those who embrace this final frontier in leadership development and embark on the Simplexity challenge find the process, as seen in my past chapters, scary yet rewarding. It is without a shadow of doubt a journey of human development which can and does achieve significant personal competitive advantage. Although in a traditional organisation, with ego and power as the key drivers, this enlightenment is also a disadvantage..... you can quickly become a mirror image of me.... Shudder at the thought!

When it is used effectively though, the process of Simplexity generates a significant return on the time and effort expended as you simply realize what energises you and what is a complete waste of time. Simplexity leadership and organisation development will always remain a complicated and challenging undertaking. Simplexity is an holistic approach which attempts to simplify and challenge while retaining the highest possible level of effectiveness and core values. A sign of your true values and ethos of Simplexity is not what you will do from now on, but what you won't do and more importantly what you say 'no' to as it doesn't fit.

Any one reading my book, will know it's not a traditional management book with structure, lessons and objectives, although I hope you gain some of these things, it's not the purpose. The purpose is to ensure change is possible, fun is vital and what ever people, academics, power and ego say...... think! You can't beat the thinker....and the thinking organisation.

The Simplexity journey will, without question, enable you as leader to work effectively in high complexity environments and to create sustainable high performance. It will not, however, change your behaviour, unless you change it today. Change begins with you, no one else will do it for you. It will help you overcome many of the problems created by reductionism by moving you into the natural, unpredictable world of individual cognition with the dynamics of life.

High performance in Simplexity is both a practical approach and a realization that whatever you do, 'shit' happens. Which in itself provides relief as a leader, so you can stop sweating the small stuff and realize that effort, energy, pride, passion, love and purpose with a high return of invested time, and resources will get you there, not knowing where there is. Simplexity is a simple view and a combination of strategy and methodology mixed with supporting elements to enable humans to add value to an organisation, in which communities, families and existence are driven and not wasting time on a pretense or act that we are in control and all- powerful over humans, nature and the world.

# Chapter 14
## "The Way We Do Things Around Here"

### Introduction:

DNA Definitive as a company has changed significantly from when I first thought about it in 1999 and I'm pleased to say it is currently expanding work across Europe and beyond, breaking away from its Welsh roots and normal business with

developments in USA, India and China, increasing our high performance ideas with change engagement efforts, aimed at meeting the demands of a 21st Century Business and removing the old 20th century management practices, which of course has a place, but not at the top or focus of the new leadership breed. I have always helped try and create an operational environment, which increases engagement, this allows smooth and constant change, creates resilience, clear purpose and a mindset that sets the Patient/Client/Service User at the front of every action and thought, by everyone in the company. Not to go over old ground, but it's the people that matter.

DNA draws on the skills and expertise of academic colleagues, associates and 'critical friends' from across UK Universities and Industrialists, providing access to a unique blend of knowledge, skills and competencies that are right for the context of the organisation: note: and I know I have said this several times so far, but its important, as we are not business consultants, as we don't offer solutions or a fixed model to apply to the issues such as Lean Systems or Six Sigma. The solutions to most organisational issues are within the business (we call them staff) and the methods must be adaptive, organic, fit for purpose and people driven. The skill is finding and engaging these solutions and with our Simplexity Architecture it's becoming easy.

At DNA we, not I, pride ourselves in providing a service that combines academic rigour, robustness, and expertise with "hands on" experience gained by working across different business sectors, not just UK based. This includes, high level sport, military and medical sectors. I always enjoy, even today, putting a Rugby Player or Surgeon in front of a group of reluctant Directors and seeing their 'what can they tell us?' attitude slip away as each story reveals another account of and perspective on leadership, decision making, purpose, failure, communication, trust etc.

DNA has an established track record of delivering large-scale leadership, 'Management Development and Change' Programmes for over 15 years now to both public and private sector organisations, including Programmes spanning a few weeks or several years providing specific skills training and coaching. The ever-growing team, comprising leadership and change agents, bring a multi-disciplinary approach to this and all our Programmes. All our 40 plus Fellows and Associates at DNA Definitive have extensive experience in the business, leadership and change arena, whilst some have all-encompassing experience in the field of higher education, bringing together a unique mix of talent, at which I have to shake myself each time I look at the list on the website. However the key factor in being part of the DNA Community is that they are able to put all of this talent into practice, not just talk, research or write about it, regardless of sector. That may sound trite but believe me, in 20 years or so of doing this, it's a rare combination.

## Our Experience

When I talk around the globe on behalf of DNA I always try to identify some of the critical success factors to delivering our methodology (way of thinking about an organisation) to develop/change, with an internal bespoke change 'ethos.' This becomes quite difficult as each organisation is unique and therefore different. In short, and without sounding like an academic I summarise this as *'taking a co-created approach'*, and some of the highlights of what we mean by this are outlined as follows:-

***The organisation will always have a specified Programme Leader for the period of the DNA intervention and beyond.*** The Programme Leader 'AN Other', will direct and help co-ordinate the delivery of the initiative. Dr Paul (me!) will add support throughout as Over-viewer, but usually it's the Programme Leader who will create the new thinking and action, and this is important as it's the internal who drives the real change, and is there when we leave to continue the movement. For all practical matters the Programme Leader will be the DNA first point of contact. This contact is daily and the change is always driven from the Programme Leader, not DNA. Although I must say here a lot rides on the PL, as if they aren't leaders, or trusted, or follow through on their promises the staff usually revert to me as default. It's a great litmus test for the issues of trust and leadership straight from the off.

*Co-Creating Intervention Systems (CCIS).* We will always work in Stages 1&2 (see example below) to 'operationalise' the brief, in order to ensure that what we propose is precisely what meets *service/staff* expectations, even though this changes consistently over the time period, in terms of outcomes, scale and prior agreed costs (costs being the immovable boundary, along with outcomes). Each stage is a 'cut-off' and reflection point as again it is important that the work is owned by the staff themselves, yet change has occurred that adds value.

*During this stage 1 in particular and 2 we create a network of ambassadors.* We consider ourselves to be ambassadors of the organisational purpose and values even when they are not so clear, but not the 'senior managers' in terms of direction or command style, when we are delivering on behalf of the organisation and fully engaged, as we feel that honesty, integrity, critical thinking and freedom are paramount to the ethos of DNA, with a sprinkling of compassion. As part of these DNA Definitive Values we arrive ready to support agreed and discovered (in our research) issues to the best of our ability, but we will always feedback honest, open and transparent information, regardless, which is quite difficult at times, but we feel necessary for progress. However with compassion we coach and mentor away problems and personal issues and create high performing, self-regulating performance for the teams. We always tailor our materials and process to the context, strategic direction and core values of trust, passion, openness, and high quality care of the organisation. This si tough, as most organisations require a model, or framework, along with detailed costs, exact outcomes and timescale...mmmmmmm tough one that for DNA. All I know is we will solve the problems, both organisationally and personally, add value to top and bottom line and leave sustainable and progressive change in place to succeed regardless.

*Commitment to evidence and continuous feed-forward improvement.* This sounds a daft statement I know for when the contract runs out we leave right?.... no not really for we ensure that what we deliver is well received by all employees even when the message is tough practical change, we commit to conducting evaluation of all our sessions, gathering pre-intervention data (Stage 1), post my/our intervention (Stage

The Award wining Leaders 2014
MoJ & Childrens Services

2) to use the findings to make even more improvements where necessary in real time. I suppose we fine-tune. We never provide the research data, the interviews, coments upfront. I did this once naively, and the management acted upon the data before we could get the staff engaged to change it themselves, and that is never the point of the research. The research at the beginning of stage 1, is simply to allow the staff to vent, feel listened to and acted upon. The issues they vent at the beginning, such as 'lack of coffee' are not often the real issues so we act on then only to show they have the power, the ability to make real, instant change. The big, real changes take place if this bit is done by us, and then in

most cases those initial moans, whinges comments disappear. Lesson learned from the off, so we never disclose those finding now, not even when threatened as I have been in several companies. We now hold the data until the organisation has changed, then present the 'this is what it use to look like/feel like before the DNA change' data, cleaned and sanitised. It's a great way to shock the now leaders not managers, as well, as most forget quite quickly what it use to look like, making the DNA seem even more miraculous (we love miracles)

*Pre-Intervention*.   I talk a lot about this stage, it the interviews with all staff, the document search, the decoration in the offices, production sheets, staff room, culture smell, the reflections of the researchers themselves.   The structure of this is listed below, however this is only a guide, which I hope will help give an insight to the emergent process and why what issues we start off with are for the most part not what we end up solving. We attempt to change and move things in accordance with the most needy issues/problems but alos allowing staff to have quick wins in the change process itself. This allows an organic, proactive and responsive process, which meets directly the needs of *the organisation* and

individuals involved in the frontline. The lift and boost in morale is simply wonderful. The energy incredible, but the increase in confidence in the frontline staff as seen here in Rob and the Team Leaders at the MoJ in 2014 is the best effect.

*Coaching.     This    is    a    key advantage for us and an open offer from* DNA Definitive as we are one of the leading proponents of coaching and mentoring. My colleague, friend and co-director Andy McCann is a genius, guru and world-class mental skills coach who works with Special Forces, Police Firearms, Surgeons, and others from the UK and beyond. He's always way too polite to say this himself, but I'm sure pays others to say it on his behalf, and they do, by the bucket loads. However, all jokes aside, the impact and change he has with 'clients' is pretty spectacular. The other guru is Steve Eaton MBE, who again makes my jaw drop and ego shrink whenever he talks about his military past, lesson learnt in the school of life and how he applies this to the business world with great effect, from changing individuals to teams to mentoring and mediation to helping Serve on and Help for Heroes. My second book will indeed explore more of this and the need for 'coaching' (I say 'coaching' but this oversimplifies what they do) for people we work with, in and out of the Simplexity process.

*With you for life.* After Stages 1 & 2 have been delivered and are in practice, we never walk away. I am quite proud that we provide an after-service, care/support, to all our clients when they need it. This can be by way of a simple telephone call, so they can receive further clarification of any key issues relating to their role and development or a  personal visit and update. We never 'walk away' from a project or client.

### Okay....What we 'normally' do in Organisations

This is what we tell our clients –

*"We will introduce employees at all levels to concepts and thinking concerned with the sustainable leadership of organisations. The speed of change and the associated complexity facing organisations in the 21st century has meant that leaders at all levels are increasingly having to develop*

*strategies and solutions which would have been considered unthinkable a few years before. In other words, leaders have more than ever before to come up with creative ideas that can be developed into successful innovations and services. While clearly this imperative can be related to new services, a crucial dimension is the harnessing of the creative abilities of employees such that the tacit knowledge they possess can be utilised to best effect. The challenge here is to develop people-driven strategies, structures, systems and cultures/climates which enable the organisation to succeed in achieving organisational 'effectiveness' and an 'advantage' within the boundaries of ever growing demands".* Its too much I know, simpler version:

We remove the management thing from the top, place into the frontline and replace with the leadership thing. We take the frontline and make them self-managing and high performing regardless of environment or culture. The combination of management at the frontline, leadership at the top, with a clear focus on purpose, values and communication creates an adaptive, thinking, fun, trusting and passionate organisation. Simple!

The 'Primary insights' research, at Stage 1, will comprise of a review of both the impact of the leadership diagnostic (the self) and further insights from within the organisation, reflection at the individual participant and organisational perspectives (truths) and will help to provide insights of perceptions, beliefs, and truths about leadership at all levels for the organisation and help provide key themes to change 'mindsets' engagement blockers/supporters.

At the **_organisational intervention_** is to help develop simultaneous the team level and bigger development and on-going reflection critical to higher performance. It will also:

- critically review organisational and leadership beliefs.

- help evidence the creation of, and 'sell' a modern organisation which facilitates on-going learning, creativity, trust and emergence of collaborative knowledge and strategic direction.

- also help facilitate real organisational structures that depict practice, responsibility, flexibility and effectiveness from frontline services upwards.

# Indicative Programme Schematic Example

Stage 1 (Start): 1-2 week duration

**Stage 1 - Pre-Programme – Specific Overview/Core Boundaries**

Stage 2: 1-2 week duration

**Health-Check & Investigation – Fact-finding**
including introduction to the process and the development of a 'Values-Contract'
Identifying key stakeholders, influencers and shapers
Programme development & draft debrief

**Individual or group work to help take forward Improvement**
**I Month - 201?**

**Stage 2 – Frontline Staff**
Simplexity 1
Understanding real practice, culture & mindset
Ground-truth, Key issues and exploring scope for development

**Stage 2a –Leadership Team**
Simplexity 2
Develop new ideas, practice change and potential solutions

**Stage 2b – Staff Change/Engagement**
Simplexity ActionShop 3
Creating multiple-micro strategies for change
Feed-forward and review

**Stage 2c – Practice & Implementation (Continual Testing)**
Coaching & Mentoring
Key staff supported and empowered with a view to sustainable personal development
Create feed-forward thinking and practice change

**Stage 3 - Feed-Forward Sessions**
**Team Coaching Sessions**
Various '*staff*' ideas to maintain core values, innovations and engagement
Creating and maintaining an ethos of confidence (whilst retaining a need for
competitive business edge), supportive change and a leadership approach to business
activities

**Stage 4 - Post-Programme Audit – The Change – Health Check – 2/6/12 month checks**

**Stage 5 OPTIONAL  - Follow up Sessions**
Guest Talks/Expert Seminars
DNA Leadership insights and community support

194

## *That's not all...*

The Simplexity Programme is based on change. Real, practical changes that enable outcomes to be achieved in a unique way where the staff feel energised and enthused about opportunities to develop the organisation. Its never done to, only done by the people having to change.

- Managers at all levels become 'leaders or strategic leaders' and engagement officers.

- HR, become talent seekers and talent supporters

- The organisation adapts faster to changing customer needs and environments.

- Engaged staff at all levels, means increased productivity with one example increasing by 300%.

- Decrease in sickness absence – 9% down in one company, 29% down in a Public Service department!

- Increased open and honest conversations allowing an increase in sustainable developments whilst decreasing conflict and waste.

- Increase in the feeling of ownership – problems solved before they escalate.

- Succession planning – helps to create the next future leaders who are cognisant of the organisation's values and 'direction of travel'

- It also turns most staff into thinking 'managers/leaders' not just employees.

- Creates a feeling of ownership and clear sense of purpose once held when the organisation was young or they had just started.


EXAMPLE
**Previous Evidenced Outcomes (2010-2014)**

1. Review and change processes to increase speed of service to clients/customers.
2. Remove barriers in communication and processes throughout the organisation.
3. Create leadership mindset to create more control and engagement for the front line staff.
4. Establish a user-led service with emphasis on an 'effective first' ethos.
5. Bring users and policy decision makers together, demystifying 'corporate speak'.
7. Understand and manage the budgets from the front line.
8. Create leaders not team managers through engagement and self-managed teams.
9. Review the quality of assessment by using peer observations not systems.
10. Invite a Senior to work day - a 'back to the floor' training schedule.

## Example Outcome Previous organisation - 1

| Change | Advantages | Benefits |
|---|---|---|
| Realignment of staff to service function, role and responsibility | Reduction of yearly financial costs without loss of service | Reduced costs Better user experience. Agile, quicker service at point of contact. Better understanding of overall corporate service needs. |
| | Working smarter which will model across departments | |

## Outcome 2

| Change | Advantages | Benefits |
|---|---|---|
| Senior Strategic Leaders, downward movement of 'management' systems & control. | Workers are seen to be trusted and developed as assets. | A more accurate use of resources. Reduced costs. Better user experience. Management as a skill pushed lower in the services. Increased quality measures. Reduced sickness/absence. |
| | Removal of duplication. | |
| | No more 'managing the system' and removal of a structure focus | |
| | Service speed improved – more agility in approach | |
| | Team Leaders allowed to coach 'back to the floor' improvements | |

## Outcome 3

| Change | Advantages | Benefits |
|---|---|---|
| 'Blending' Services - Teams seamlessly into all areas of the service | Better use of resources. | Reduced costs. Improved user experience. Improved retention in front contact services. |
| | Better use of finances. | |
| | Service speed improved. | |
| | Less duplication. | |

# Background – Theory

*The Emergence of Complex Evolving Systems Leadership Approach*

Complexity science or the DNA version of **Simplexity** is not mainstream in the management curricula or practice but  is an emergent discipline in both areas. The study of complexity science and complex evolving systems is still embryonic, but we have encountered through the direct work of DNA widespread interest amongst senior managers and policy makers, keen to explore these principles in managing their organisations in the 21st Century. Pockets of relevant expertise have emerged within the UK and HEIs enabling us to build a dispersed network of expertise which we can draw in flexibly as required. Complexity science has many concepts within its aegis. See Figure 1.

## Figure 1.

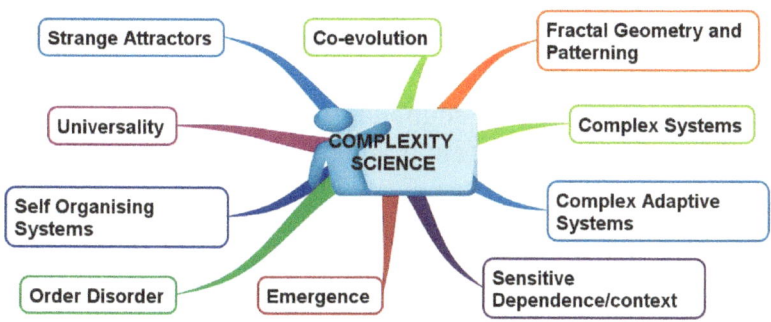

Outside the hard sciences two major complexity science strands have emerged:

1. Complex systems research –involving the mathematical study of interacting agents in complex hierarchies producing unpredictable outcomes. Funding has been attracted from research bodies to engage in IT, robotics and socio-technical systems modelling projects.

2. **Simplexity**–the focus of this project, takes concepts out of the scientific domain and develops applications in social leadership functions. It focuses on complex living systems (humans) which learn (as opposed to react) in response to internal and external environmental changes. It addresses human dynamics and responsive processes. It does not subscribe to the control paradigm (and is therefore difficult to fund).

Discoveries in the living sciences offer many insights into how complex living systems are designed and adapt to changing circumstances. Using this knowledge we can better understand how to manage complex adaptive systems like organisations, but this knowledge challenges the assumptions of Newtonian-Cartesian science which underpinned the industrial revolution and 'scientific management'. In the 20th century, this paradigm of thinking was challenged by quantum physics and then by developments in chaos and complexity science. In the field of management, 'complexity thinking' offers the promise of a new management science. **See figure 2.**

**Figure 2**: Traditional and Complexity Thinking about Organizations and Research: Comparing Paradigms

| Traditional Management | 21st Century Leadership |
|---|---|
| *Essentially mechanistic* | *Essentially dynamic / self organising* |
| Linear | Non linear |
| Controllable | Uncontrollable |
| Centralised | Networked |
| Hierarchical | Non hierarchical |
| Limited connectivity | Highly connected |
| Uniformity | Diversity |
| Cause and Effect | Effect and Effect |
| Predictable | Unpredictable |
| Reductionist | Holistic |
| Objective explanation | Subjective & Objective explanation |
| Entity focussed | Process focused |
| Correlation | Patterning |
| Highly preclusive | Highly inclusive |
| Evolutionary | Revolutionary & 'New' Evolutionary |

(Adapted from Kelly 2004, McMillian 2008 and Thomas 2010)

The application of **Simplexity**, offers new concepts, innovations and a different lens through which to explore organisational change issues and leadership requirements in more challenging environments. This project caters for the *emergence* of themes from the frontline staff themselves in any given organisational context and the interdependencies between elements in a system, which lead to successful adaptation. The theory of **Simplexity** (making the Complexity, simple, hence Simple-xity) allows the creation of an architecture, a human framework that allows the people within, the people who make a  product or provide a service to change according to this architecture to create the new organisation from the people/service needs upwards. Or in my utopia, downwards. Managers get paid less, if you can remember way back in chapter 1.

## *Leaders as Human Builders*

Okay the following is the basis of my work in terms of academic research, theory, philosophy and methodology. Still awake? Well you won't be in a moment! I would normally put references after each sentence to prove how well read I am, and that, more truthfully, this work, my work, is not new, it's the culmination of hundreds of years of research and thinking. The new bit is perhaps that I put 'it' into practice, but again, humans have been around for a while, and it's only 'management' which is 'new' worn out, and failing. So I'll say it here... the following is as a result of some great authors such as Drucker, Mintzberg, Pascale, McMillian, Mitleton-Kelly, Kauffman, Bourdieu, etc. I could go on. Rather than do the normal academic writing thing, it's easier for you the reader if you can just skip to the References at the back to see the influences and authors of the following. I have tried to simplify their writing and work...... and hope you find it an okay section (i.e. not too academic or boring).

DNA's strategy of Simplexity can be used by any individual, at any level of an organisation, in any formal or informal position. Each individual (latent leader) has a capacity to influence all situations they interact with to some extent. An individual's potential for influence will depend on their formal and informal position in the organisation. Senior leaders are more likely to be able to initiate change efforts

202

supported by external support such as a DNA member and supplemented with training. Individuals at frontline are more likely to only have themselves and what they are personally able to impact whilst providing the service or product. Each frontline leader's situation has a set of limits constraining what they are able to do, and this can be real or perceived. The challenge for each leader is to maximise their impact within these constraints, after we help realise them via the training in Simplexity. We also, at each stage of the process, help to remove the constraints in the system to help build trust and reflection points as stated above. This is normally by removing the frustration points and providing simple stuff such as a new phone or an upgraded note pad to write on. It is that simple.

Implementing a whole system development programme from any field of study or perspective, requires some positioning which has a high 'value adding' impact and is important for leaders at all levels to use as a conduit to aid the change process. This role involves taking action to understand, design, create and transform all forms of organisational entity to improve performance and viability. I sometimes call them CHR Officers (Chef Hurdle Removers). As leaders are inherently part of the systems being developed, the development process also means developing themselves and their own practice as well as some part of the organisation, which is tough. I rarely find that leaders, regardless of age or ability, who are willing to change. There is always a fear that once the change happens they will not process the skills or attitude to cope. The fear of being exposed is tangible and real in some instances.

Peter Drucker 'the' guru in Management states that 'managerialism' should not be viewed as the dominant discourse which, through authoritative and benevolent management, it seeks power and control might which no longer is appropriate or as the only approach to diversity in organisations. Human active systems (organisations) are in reality nonlinear, messy and operate as an interactive tribal community characterised by the potential for self-organisation, people forming their own groups, which exist in a non-stable environment regardless of what we perceive as non-changing. This, if accepted, simply allows people such as those in the frontline to help create a service from the immediate need upwards.   In truth, (and there is only truth....no such thing as fact, as even facts need to be explained) organisations are unscientific, simply because they are human and evolving, contributed to by problems, crises and messy service provision with increasing diversity, behaviours and multi-culturalism, amongst other issues.

The 'messy' ill-defined perspective of the nature of organisations and the apparent 'irrational' behaviour of the humans operating within them all add  to the call  for a new way of doing things in organisation. It also demonstrates the move towards and use of metaphors to describe and understand the world that we live within, which is, according to many, increasing in complication due to globalisation. I want to call this world Simplexity!

The terminology of management, structure and control will always be used, even throughout my work, simply to help in the development of the change needed, that managerialism is counter-intuitive to *successful* organisation, whatever successful actually means to the individual. As a result, it is inevitable that new and "increasing differences" will contribute to a larger inventory of issues in organisations, ranging from small day-to-day problems, through to a 'blue-print' of much larger organisational operation.   Mess is here to stay and long live the mess, as it's where creativity, invention and fun happen.

## *Managerialism is dead. Long live Gardening!*

When critically reflecting upon the dominant theory of management discourse in the context of management, I state often that the traditional discourse is hegemonic - relying upon power, control, certainty and uniformity and the promotion of self-interest in its daily operation. It is therefore out-dated as an approach to dealing with people in organisations. Classical management principles and "Taylorism" have fuelled managerialism from the first scientific renaissance. From these principles emerged the "machine organisation" where "take, make and break" predominated. In this type of environment, resources are taken and converted to products and services, i.e. creating a way of doing which limits the innovation at the frontline.

Let's quickly critique both the impact of the dominant theory of 'managerialism' on the micro-level management speak as well as revealing the theoretical position of Simplexity as an alternative paradigm for any leader in the frontline. I will not suggest here nor do I ever, that Simplexity should or could permanently replace managerialism as a dominant discourse, but merely present Simplexity as an alternative philosophy/perspective for consideration when dealing with leadership, people, problems and therefore leading people in organisations. By so doing, new possibilities and solutions may help the human interaction of agents external to and within the problem, leadership and organisation.

## People as 'Agents' in organisations – Power to the People!

Simplexity focuses on people as individual agents who have the freedom to act in ways that are not always totally predictable and whose actions are interconnected, such as one agent's actions changing the context for the other agents. Agents therefore thrive on a consultative and participative style and good communications, transparency and trust as prerequisites for successful social networking. Connectivity between the agents especially within the "web of increasing differences" emerges and co-evolves within the organisation and is the primary focus of the Simplexity 'manager' or 'gardener'. The 'gardener' of the organisation, by concentrating on maintaining and increase the effective social web, communication and knowledge transfer, builds trust, openness, and acceptance of risk, and aids quicker response rates for action.

Agents (people with power, realised or not) are considered as independent and freethinking individuals that form part of an organisation and possibly support and share the organisational value and ethos. Agents are innovators and entrepreneurs who are prepared and allowed to take risks in their quest to develop a new order. Agents are intuitive and inquisitive and are problem solvers in circumstances of problems, direction and operations. I sometimes see these agents manifest themselves in strange places in the organisation, including the 'awkward' ones who have been seen as trouble makers or non-responsive to the future work. I call these people the 'Denise's' of the organisation as it reminds me of the work at one factory and a lady who was trouble. She was awkward, negative and downright abusive at times, well to me anyhow. However, when she actually got what we were trying to do, change and remove, in her words get rid of the 'crap', wow... things changed overnight, and so did the organisation. It was a joy to see this 'awkward' mostly miserable employee become switched on and excited.

Simplexity thinking accepts organisations as a Human Active mess, by definition. Agents are valued as key to delivering better, adaptive and more responsive systems and are trusted to think, act and do. Agents are people that must therefore share in, develop and maintain the evolving value of the organisation. This again falls fowl of some organisations who talk engagement, yet design policies, structures and purpose behind closed doors, and then wonder why people (agents) don't empower or drive their thinking.

Simplexity thinking emerges as an alternative life-science model, like a species in a new ecological niche. Complexity? is organic and promotes an alternative philosophy to 'machine managerialism', control and prediction and suggests that people constantly (regardless if given permission) "innovate, proliferate and aggregate". Here we think nature appears to favour adaptation, where most species compete when faced with adversity. Innovation in a Simplexity organisation stems from open democracy, risk acceptance and trust through boundaries and purpose for it to work. Proliferation is the survival of the fittest and this survival relies on how much faster you can reproduce or emerge new order (new ways of doing things) than can your competitors. Arthur calls this phenomenon "increasing returns" and aggregation is the delivery of these 'increasing returns' in sheer strength of numbers (Arthur 2002). The more we try the better the results and the more people then start to innovate, the more

207

the organisation becomes adaptive, responsive and sustaining. Simplexity!

## *The Recognition of the role of diversity in organisations*

Diversity is the organisation's life-blood and is without doubt, at the heart of any organisation's cultural web, paradigms, mind-sets and values, irrespective of what any authoritative or autocratic discourse would suggest. Diversity drives emergence through human and social systems within organisations and therefore helps delivery through emancipatory and adaptive, bottom-up approach operating only within boundaries that will help meet emerging organisational needs, normally defined as 'goals' or 'targets'.

I state often that the traditional discourse of managerialism and that of Simplexity, recognise the need for diversity in organisations especially when dealing with people. When an organisation's form is a diverse web of ages, gender, race and religions, cultures, etc. then it is inevitable that this can lead to behavioural issues and problems that can impact upon rational objectives and strategy formulation. However, where the two discourses appear to be at odds is that 'classical managerialism' assumes it has the power, control and therefore the authority to, in any situation, 'manage' issues, problems and future crises that may arise from this diverse culture. However, in Simplexity and Simplex organisations, diversity gives way to fun, ideas, thoughts, cross-stimulation, and emergent order, usually seen at the end point of a product delivery/service. It also removes the silly notion that rationality actually exists in an organisation in the first place.

208

Problems stated above are simply opportunities to think, question and direct.

I also state at every possible point that people pretend to listen to others, but rarely fail to hear what is being said, by the person talking. That it was not from the organisational machine and planning that a new order emerged in the face of these events, but the social interaction of people (agents) that emerged as a result of the interconnectivity and interdependence from the operation. The more we get people to understand their role, where they fit and what they do in adding value to the service or product the better the organisation works. The mechanistic, silo mentality found in most organisations just removes the focus on the customer, putting in its place a focus of protecting itself. Think HR or Finance and how, despite the lovely, happy people within each department, they eventually do that builders' mantra of a deep , sigh,  before telling us all the reason why something cannot happen, without great cost or law breaking.

Simplexity as an alternative discourse is therefore necessary to posit an emergent and transforming view of leading a human social system, in a world where fast or quick solutions appear to dominate cultures and organisational strategies. Traditionally, the dominant, scientific discourse typically attempts to do this, through rational, 'reductionist' systems, which attempt to manage people like machines or cogs in a machine. Simplexity views managers as "gardeners" an analogy which attempts to remove power and coercion, found in the notion of Managerialism,  and replace them with influence, cultivation and nurture fostering the correct response at the point of need, "exploring the space of possibilities" in a consultative and participative style. Stacey (2004) also suggests that Simplexity is the magnet that helps agents as well as 'gardeners' to inquire and challenge established management mind-sets and discourses. So here Simplexity helps us view an organisation which is moving away from a classical management view which is counter-intuitive, to a more human focused approach.

Simplexity, using Mitleton-Kelly's (2003) framework and a DNA methodology, forms the 'magnets for this inquiry'. This framework expounds a fitting methodology to develop and conceptualise the reality of dealing with human diversity and crisis in organisations. We continue to suggest that Simplexity constructs a powerful argument that this is how the organisation actually operates regardless of belief systems. Simplexity provides the basis on which adaptation and evolution become the new ethos and guiding principles of organisations for the 21st century and beyond.

Applying Simplexity within our work and organisational context serves to illustrate that organisations can achieve 'increasing (strategic) intellectual capital returns' through defining or setting boundaries and creating new cultures and paradigms. Simplexity centres on a human relations perspective towards organisational diversity and crises through empowerment and divesting control, trust and integrity, resulting in increased ownership and shared values by the workforce. Our work advocates that Simplexity is a catalyst for organisational and functional change, demonstrating that Simplexity may improve effectiveness and organisational democracy, cutting across the functional boundaries, allowing 'self-organisation', developing improved communication, granting employees opportunities to 'explore the space of possibilities'.

As a result, this alternative discourse of, Simplexity, could only be 'emergent' in nature i.e. you can be aware and prepare for problematic situations but you cannot control them even by having engaged and frontline focussed provision through democratic leadership. We also suggest that management stop attempting to control the future and concentrate more on controlling their reaction to given situations which emerge through frontline services, thereby contributing to the 'creation of a new order', taking the organisation through to a state "far from its original equilibrium" within the boundaries of, for example, finance, quality, performance.

In addition, we Simplexity thinkers view managerialism and its persistent search for equilibrium,  as silly in human systems.  A human system can never be in a state of equilibrium because elements are always unfolding and in transition.  As a result the search for equilibrium is simply death, not stability.  Managerialism infers stability and complacency, plus uniformity and conformity which is a counter-intuitive style that kills long-term effectiveness and in the end the organisation itself, or parts of it. Although, it is important that organisations build in rest- points, reflection and chances to re-energise, for at times the people have to sprint to achieve high performance and as we all know quite well, the Olympic sprinter takes a lot of rest in-between high performance races.

## Systems Thinking Plus+ = Simplexity

Systems Thinking is not new, and Vanguard is not the only approach. The principles of systems thinking have been known and around for decades,  as the first real studies in Soft Systems began in 1962. Key thinkers like Isaac Newton, and

Albert Einstein have been accused of using system thinking in their work many times, and most in education will W. Edwards Deming, the management quality guru was a systems user and systems thinker who claimed that 95% of performance issues are attributable to the "system", such as work flow, structure, management, processes, measures, customers, etc. with just 5% attributable to individuals. What's funny here is that in 2010, about 2 minutes before I went on stage to talk to a group of students, a well known author who claims to have invented Systems Thinking phoned me. Now let's say that having listened to him several times and read his books, oh, and watched his videos, which he incidentally plays in his lectures (which I find quite eerie) I would always feel a little awkward knowing that his claims to be the inventor of Systems Thinking Methodology were, well, over- exaggerated. I would often revisit the groups who would be desperate to tell me what he had claimed, and me, being me, would go into the long history of Systems Thinking. Well! The world being as it is, small, this got back to him and resulted in the phone call, as I say, as I was just about to step onto the stage. Let's say he swore a lot, promised to rearrange my 'Welsh' ears, regardless of the fact that I was a rugby player, and come down immedietely from his ivory tower to do so if I told another person that his method was old, and invented many, many years ago. Now I wouldn't normally tell people about the abusive telephone calls I receive, but on this occasion I managed to move onto the stage and place the phone next to the microphone for all to hear. Wrong, I know, , but so funny. My student ratings and legend levels went high that day.

Needless to say he did get me back several years later, when he was invited to do a debate with Dave Snowden and me, in Cardiff for the CEO's of major companies and organisations.

Neither he, nor Dave Snowden turned up. It is now known as the 'Event we shall never speak of,' as I was left trying to hold a debate with 120 CEO's, who, let's face it, would rather have been somewhere else.

Systems thinking as we know originated in the 1920s within several disciplines, notably biology and engineering. It was an attempt to use scientific methods (such as, reduction, repeatability and refutation) to understand, and of course control, by breaking things down into their constituent parts and exploring the properties of these parts so that they could be understood and rebuilt in a way that benefits the organisation. People thought and claimed that Systems Thinking, albeit a little crude, if broken down correctly, would one day be the core method to help design, control and improve all organisations.

Systems thinking does helps us to see the inter-relationships between things, as well as the underlying patterns and possible root-causes of symptoms that occur every day in organisations. Its claim and mantra about finding practical, effective and sustainable solutions to a myriad of real-world problems, even with complicated issues, is, at the face of it, correct(ish). The majority , use "systems thinking" because it means they are better able to understand what makes things the way they are and to understand the constraints, boundaries and connections that together create a specific output. This includes, and this is where it loses me, the culture and mindsets, to clarify and consider the 'holistic' view of what we do from the inside.

Systems Thinking ensures that any possible interventions made by staff address the real underlying causes, rather than just dealing with the symptoms. An example here I often talk about is the Sickness & Absenteeism Policy found in most companies. The HR people will normally have 'back to work' interviews, off work checks on the employee procedures, punishment, sorry review interviews for people off sick in any form of pattern etc. etc. Systems, on the otherhand, attempts to consider and focus on the reason why they went on the sick in the first instance and recognise a pattern if lots are off from the same section. Systems helps us ask better questions rather than it coming up with solutions simply because it attempts to focus in on the whole system rather than one specific part of it.

So, Systems Thinking has not failed nor is it wrong per se, it has been just set inappropriate expectations by consultants and over zealous Systems thinkers, in a way, building it up to fail. The key issue for me apart from the over zealous Consultants who use Systems, even their own 'versions,' in inappropriate areas is the failure to understand that they are dealing with individuals and subjectivity, and the personal capacity to transform any complex theory into simple working language is extremely difficult. It doesn't matter, who you are speaking to, or that they are hyper-intelligent or just plain un-motivated, they will all have a 'take' on what they think 'Systems' is, and hope it applies to them, and this changes constantly with time.

Whilst, if you accept that decision-makers who are throughout the organisation work from sense-making, co-evolutions, interaction, and reflection, since making and so on, few will ever attend a workshop on systems, but gain a second hand view of the theory, which will alter over each conversation, use and time. You only have to think of the game 'Chinese Whispers' to understand what I mean in this instance.

214

Systems Theory and even the added academic theories on Complexity are largely ignored in the heat of action and practice, replaced by subjective, historical thinking and immediacy. Deep core values and behaviour are relied upon when reactive responses are required, as they are simply tried and tested and possibly risk adverse.

The other issue for me with Systems is "What is a system?" This is best answered by Checkland, one of the key authors on Systems: ..."*A system is a set of elements, connected together, which form a whole; this showing properties which are properties of the whole rather than of its component parts.*"(Checkland, 1962). In the 1990s (late) Systems was made more accessible to practising managers and others, largely by Peter Senge from the work of people like Checkland et al. One of the key contributions of this has been the identification of systems archetypes i.e. influence patterns that can be found in many different systems. Yet, along the way, the term whole systems and Systems has become misapplied, and is now commonly used instead of the term system-wide.

The development of Complexity and for that matter Chaos Theory has demonstrated that the early Systems Thinkers, and that abusive Systems Consultant (see above) were over ambitious, and again zealous in their belief that the dynamics of a human 'system' (there is a strong argument that humans are not in a system – freewill, etc. but we will leave that for book two) could be analysed and detailed, let alone understood. We know that complex, dynamic human systems can be extremely sensitive to initial starting conditions, the butterfly effect wing over the china for example, and that such a system is unlikely to yield to analysis in this way or prediction in detail. So why try? Okay, don't answer that one....

This doesn't mean that Systems is no longer useful, or that it has been superseded by complexity theory. Indeed DNA is proudly a Systems Thinking organisation and it is a key part of our methodology. It is a vital component of complexity theory as practice as the diagram from Eve Mitleton-Kelly wonderfully illustrated. It is therefore an element of Complexity but not, as some mistakenly assume, Complexity itself. One of the biggest assumptions I see in organisations and change initiatives is that we assume everyone naturally sees the problems the way we see them, and therefore can easily switch to using our viewpoint (tools and concepts) to address the problem, rather than seeing what actually exists as the issue.

We also have to remember that if the problem in today's organisations is the 'non-human' view or management model, then Systems Thinking reinforces the view that people are 'cogs' in the machine and once cleaned (trained), they will act according to the machine schema. Systems will not address the problem that management is about control, reductionism and power. It is does not matter how well Systems Theory is introduced to an organisation, without first getting the agents/staff/managers to understand the human aspect, the Systems will always fail in time.

We also assume linear and clear understanding of the original problem. You only have to watch the film Memento to understand the world is not simple, reducible to facts or linear. We like to use the phrase "This analysis provides evidence that....", which again usually homes in on the symptom to describe a situation that may have complex, interactive, messy causes, which cannot be explained at the moment of 'analysis'. You only have to get a team to work on an issue to realise that the story changes with time.

216

## Complexity Theory – Simplexity!

Complexity (Simplexity) has emerged as a 'new' theoretical approach to organisational analysis and is beginning to attract the attention of social work practitioners and scholars. Indeed as I have stated, 10 years ago, very few companies would allow me in, let alone listen to my views, yet today DNA is a growing and much copied force. Simplexity, draws from and builds on many of the key principles within Systems, as it shares with Systems the fundamental challenge to the traditional linear cause-and-effect thinking, and uses the concepts of emergence, connectivity, interdependence and feedback, described in more detail below. However, it is argued by its proponents that it does not suffer the same limitations as general Systems Thinking in quantifying social concerns over time and location. Simplexity, unlike Systems, theorises the 'systems' as complex co-evolving networks – in my words, 'messy'. Simplexity, goes beyond Systems in that it recognises, not just that component parts within a system are related and will have an effect on each other, but also that in open systems (human) the effects are not predictable, are prone to change and require a more intuitive approach from practitioners.

The word complexity is derived from the Latin *complexus* meaning intertwined. Simplexity argues that complex behaviour arises from the connectivity and interaction between systems and their environments. Decisions or actions by one individual or system have the potential to impact on other related individuals and systems. The extent or nature of any impact is not predictable and will be neither uniform nor equal. It varies depending on the state of each system and each system's state is dependent on factors including its history, structure and organisational impact.

Simplexity is an emerging paradigm in the workplace. Human systems are inherently complex and any work is inherently a 'simplexity profession' in that it attempts to take account of and respond to the complexities people encounter in real life, there we go with the mess again. Human behaviour is unpredictable (messy) and people can change their rules of interaction and expected outcomes, more mess. Given the diversity of problems, relationships and biographical narratives encountered by staff at the frontline, simplexity thinking may, therefore, be a helpful framework for professions, from teachers right through to Binmen (or should that be 'Binpersons', or Refuse Officers)

Simplexity, has now spread from the analysis of clients and users to that of the organisations, which service them as it suggests that rather than being seen as structural machines, customers, institutions and organisations should be understood as much more complex, evolving and messy, that operate and co-evolve within what Mitleton-Kelly refers to as a social 'ecosystem'. If organisations like local authorities and work teams are understood from this perspective then this provides alternative ways of acting and relating that bring with them the potential for different and potentially more effective forms of management, strategy, decision-making and acceptance of risk.

There is no single unified theory of simplexity, as it draws from various natural sciences, mathematics and physics. Simplexity is a conceptual framework or architecture, rather than a particular methodology. For the purposes of this explanation I shall be relying on Mitleton-Kelly's ten principles

218

of complexity in providing a simple, yet brilliant framework for understanding. Mitleton-Kelly's work is based on research examining the implications for organisations of the generic characteristics set out here. Since my work is looking at the application of Complexity and its implications for organisational effectiveness, it therefore provides a useful starting point in the explanation of the world of DNA.

The ten principles identified by Mitleton-Kelly as being generic characteristics of Simplexity are: **connectivity, interdependence, co-evolution, far-from-equilibrium, historicity, path-dependence, exploration-of-the-space-of-possibilities, feedback, self-organisation and emergence.** Simplexity, argues that it is not enough to take any one of these characteristics in isolation. In order to achieve an understanding of the organisation, it is necessary to look at the characteristics together and to take account of the holistic view, otherwise we would fall into the world of reductionism again.

Mitleton-Kelly's seminal work in 2000 argues that, whilst all the principles she identifies are generic to all natural complex systems, the distinguishing characteristic of a Simplexity is its ability to create new order through adaptation/co-evolution. Individuals acting according to their own agendas can work effectively as a group to create coherence, new order, structures or ways of working without any apparent overall strategy or design.

## *Connectivity and interdependence* ♣

The term 'connectivity' relates to how people within an organisation are connected to each other and how systems themselves are connected. High connectivity requires a high level of interdependence but this will not automatically produce positive benefits. Interdependence between systems means that as one system evolves and changes it effects changes on connected systems. The higher the interdependence, the greater the chances are of disturbance from other connected systems;

> 'When one entity tries to improve its fitness or position, this may result in a worsening condition for others. Each 'improvement' in one entity therefore may impose associated 'costs' on other entities, either within the same system or on other related systems.' (Mitleton-Kelly, 2002, p4)

Many state that biological ecosystems are not fully connected. Each species typically interacts with a limited number of other species, although again the butterfly effect is always present. Likewise, in human systems, there are networks of relationships (tribes) with different degrees of connectivity. Individuals may be connected to many different groups; the impact any individual has will depend not only on that individual but also on the others within the group. This degree of connectivity varies over time and is dependent on the diversity, intensity and quality of interactions and so it is not uniform, constant or predictable. You only have to think of the people you work with and know how you connect with some,

---

♣ These terms are considered the architecture of Human Systems

a little with others and 'not really' with a few. The degree of connectivity will determine the network of relationships, which in turn determines the creation, strength and sharing of information and knowledge. However, you must also understand that sometimes if you have a power 'freak' in the tribe, knowledge becomes a source of protection, status and ego. That's difficult to break and the 'Connectivity' becomes a veneer with no depth or foundation upon which to build sustainability.

## *Co-evolution*

Co-evolution describes the dependence of one agent on the evolution of other related agents (people), the changes that each experiences in the context of other people and how the changes they are experiencing merge out of the relationship and impact. Each agent is influenced by, and influences, the human. Change from a Simplexity perspective is therefore not the result of a system or procedure or process but the people adapting o each other as they connect and emerge. Human relationships are not isolated and unidirectional but reciprocal, messy and connected. Managers should not, therefore, make definitive responses to changing environments but must understand that the decisions it takes will affect the social ecosystem it operates within.

## *Far-from-equilibrium, historicity and path-dependence*

The term 'far-from-equilibrium' stems from Prigogine's work on cell formation. According to Prigogine, far-from-equilibrium states are those subjected to energy causing the system to move from stability, and ultimately, to evolve and create new order. Prigogine, (1996). This is the order-disorder-order pattern found in human systems. The fact that what ultimately occurs is not predictable and is only one of a range of possible occurrences creates a historical dimension. The concept has been transferred to the social sciences to describe the type of equilibrium in which human life exists, that is, an environment subject to volatile, and unanticipated changes. Assumptions are often made that the most desirable state for an organisation is one of equilibrium, where acting influences cancel each other out, resulting in a stable and unchanging system. Simplexity argues that systems in equilibrium stagnate. Creating disorder to de-stabilise a system pushes it far-from-equilibrium and enables transformational change to occur (Byrne, 1998).

Historical events are conventionally assumed to move in a linear, cause-and-effect direction and when viewed in hindsight this is how things appear. At DNA we argue, however, that in reality this is not the case. An individual may make a series of decisions from a range of possible alternatives. Each decision determines a particular path, referred to as 'path-dependence'. Future choices are constrained by the individual's current state and the environment they live in. The emergent behaviour is not coincidental but the result of their past decisions (the history), current environment and on-going choices, and so this goes on. Subsequent evolution may be dependent on the particular decision made, so that the making of that decision creates a historical element. However, up to the point that a decision is finalised, the possible alternatives remain as sources of innovation and diversification. When an entity is confronted with a barrier to survival, it is forced to experiment and find alternative ways of working (Mitleton-Kelly, 2002). The fact that far-from-equilibrium systems are evolving entities means that the way they behave cannot be predicted from an examination of past behaviour. If this is the case, then strategic planning based on direct extrapolation from past experience is daft.

Although organisations can be deliberately pushed into a state of far-from-equilibrium to bring about new order, we do this as part of DNA stage 1 and 2, attempting to design new order in detail risks limiting the possibilities for self-organisation. We have witnessed over the past 15 years that change managers often unintentionally limit or constrain emergent behaviour by attempting to control outcomes via objectives, pre-conditions and flawed communication without 'trust' or engagement. Organisation re-design should always focus on creating the conditions that enable the emergence of new ways of working from the frontline upwards. It's the only way to ensure a continued service/product and value added.

> 'If organisation re-design were to concentrate on the provision of *enabling infrastructures* ... allowing new patterns of relationships and ways of working to emerge, new forms of organisation may arise that would be unique ... . These new organisational forms may be more robust and sustainable in competitive environments.' (Mitleton-Kelly, 2002, p.14).

## Exploration of the space of possibilities

The search for a single perfect solution is without question, in Simplexity terms, neither desirable nor possible. To thrive, an entity needs to explore the space of possibilities and create variety, like the humans themselves being all different and individual. The perfect solution will only be perfect for a particular time and set of circumstances and people. I have often explained this by the use of Lean Systems Thinking, created in a Japanese manufacturing plant by a group of workers. My Knicker Factory Wales does not have Japanese workers in it..... it will never be the same Lean Systems process regardless. As those people change so the solution that was ideal is likely to become less fit-for-purpose. If the environment an organisation is operating within is dynamic and unstable then the organisation itself needs to be flexible.

## Feedback process

A feedback loop is formed when an event occurs in an environment to which a system responds, and that response has an effect back on the agents. This effect then forms a new event, to which there is a further response. Positive feedback amplifies/reinforces the impact of an action and drives change. Negative feedback balances or moderates it, thus maintaining stability. Numerous feedback loops can be in operation at any given time. From an organisational perspective negative feedback includes monitoring and quality assurance processes, positive feedback includes information from outside its system. Far-from-equilibrium conditions are created when a system is pushed beyond established ways of working. At a certain point the pressure on the system becomes critical, which can cause the organisation to collapse into disorder and lead to the 'creation of new order'. The feedback process can amplify small changes, exacerbating the pressure towards underlying transformation, becoming the butterfly effect and the moment at the cliff. Feedback processes are of course messy and non-linear, the inputs and outputs are unpredictable due to the effects of connectivity, time and context.

## *Self-organisation, emergence and creation-of-new-order*

A human system needs to be studied as a whole and cannot be understood by reduction to its constituent parts. This we learned from Checkland, 1981. In Simplexity, the agents are interacting with each other, acting according to their own rules without apparent co-ordination. People within organisations adapt their own behaviour and actions in parallel with feedback about the actions and behaviour of others. This is what Simplexity refers to as 'self-organisation'. It is the spontaneous order that arises from the interaction of individual elements to create something greater than the sum of its parts. Within an organisational context self-organisation describes how agents can come together to achieve a purpose with no external direction;

> 'This component reflects an organization's ability to respond to the emerging preferences of the clients who chose to participate in that organization. It also reflects the ability of the agents to self-organise into self-help groups.' (Wolf-Branigin, 2009, p. 199)

Whether self-organisation will occur, how it will manifest or what it will achieve is not predictable.

Emergence is a characteristic of all human interaction. It is a product of context relationships and interactions where the responses of individuals lead to the emergence of larger systems. I also think there is an impact even in loose-coupled situations. You only have to think of a nasty comment on Twitter by a Troll (think that's the correct term) to feel the impact. Simplexity suggests that, although behaviour appears to emerge in a seemingly chaotic way, it is actually responding to the architecture of complexity. For example, teams working to identical structures and organisational requirements may act in entirely different ways. This cannot be predicted or understood from the behaviour or properties of the individuals.

## Complexity Theory and the Public Sector

Simplexity can be applied to both the complicated worlds that any organisation inhabits with its staff, and the needs of customers. Simplexity may provide a framework for dealing with problem situations that are not easily defined, have no definite solutions and where there is a high human activity component such as is characteristic of any frontline workers, working with customers. The possibilities offered for exploring the space of possibilities, understanding co-evolution and seeking not a 'right' answer but possible and relevant answers - situational thinking, has demonstrated huge potential and actual practice to help Leaders' understanding of the current state of the organisation and its effectiveness.

There is little currently written on the practical application of complexity and how it might add value to practice. I am perhaps a little to blame on this as all the companies and organisations we've worked with over the past 15 years, I've not made the effort to place them in the academic world. Why? Well I think deep down the rules and acceptance needed to get published in those all important journals never really excited me. It was a loop too far to jump in my academic life. But hey, I've done Radio and BBC TV to get the message out there!

Although there is only limited academic literature on Simplexity practice and data, with its focus on achieving change through practice-based change, learning and reflection, we are finding this a useful approach within organisations. Simplexity is a methodology and an approach to inquiry and change that supports many methods and can therefore be combined with all sorts of ideas and thoughts, including differing schools of thought, such as in-depth interviews, rich pictures, open questionnaires and a wide range of other methods. Simplexity because of its participatory nature, and its concern with open systems and emergent behaviour, recognises the messiness of social human interaction and so its incredibly difficult to predict, guess the future and certainly not plan!

# Appendix

# Example - The DNA Programme

**DNA Mandate:**

- Employee Engagement – immediate change – normally 2-4 weeks
- 21st Century Leadership Practice throughout as a Pilot study
- Creating an "Immediate Change" from frontline up
- Help embed 'The Way Things are Done Around Here' core value as practice

**Project scope: decided by the engagement with the frontline and customers...but this is a first stab**

- Create a full staff engagement across the service to identify opportunities/ambitions/values and perceived or actual blocks to taking the service forward.
- Help to redesign several areas simultaneously to allow Senior Managers to understand progress, change methodology and 'difference' in the project 'The Way Things are Done Around Here' ethos.
- Create connectivity and interdependence – value recognition in 21st Century leadership in the Pilot areas.

**Core outcomes: Yep!**

- To deliver a set of key themes and associated quick wins that will re-energise a sense that the service is moving in the right direction and that this direction is in line with people's core values.
- Create a shared values set to support sharing and from corporate communications to produce the 'new' ethos.
- Internal Change 'Champions' driving the shared values and service innovations.

**Constraints: (mmmm not sure we think of these at times)**

- Government Guidelines/Legal Mandates/Regulations will be adhered to throughout.

**Assumptions: (dangerous we know, but hey we have to)**

- Full commitment by the Senior Management Team.
- Clear information and dissemination of information as requested.
- Commitment to engagement and the notion of frontline empowerment

**Project approach: Always..... no, not really... but it's a start**

- Full participation and continuous coaching throughout Stage One.
- Create frontline disruption and Team Leader deconstruction techniques unique to DNA.
- Create democratic, customer-driven systems and thinking to adapt faster than anyone else or previously seen in the organisation.
- Removal of frustrations and nonsense to become more effective with resources (human and financial).
- Create an internal Team of Change Agents from the frontline upwards. Engagement.
- Ensure as many as possible realise and understand that change is based on theoretical approach, but occurs always from a practice/operational perspective.
- Subjective ontology, so the individual becomes the focus of change, not the system, process or rule.

**Project tolerances: we try not to, honest!**

- No disruption to internal/external customers' service.
- No increase in costs or expenditure during the programme or as a result of the programme.
- No increase in defect/product failure stats.
- No loss of staff as a result of the programme.

**21st Century Leadership – tangible results**
*(As documented by the BBC in six Programmes):*

## *When you change the DNA you get?....*

An increase in Trust within the organisation to **91%** (Pembrokeshire Engineering, 2006)

An increase in the feeling of empowerment in staff by **94%** (Turbine Company Europe, 2006-2008)

Staff and Leaders increase to improve service/outputs **up 87%** (Welsh City Council Social Services, 2009)

The drive by all staff to "deliver a 'Good Service'" **up 89%** (BGCBC – Maintenance, 2010)

**Savings in excess of 40% without job losses** (BGCBC - recycling and bin collection, 2010)

**Increase in Profit margins 10-28%** (Clothing Factory, 2010)

**Reduction in Waste min 31%** (South Wales Manufacturing Company, 2013)

# References used in the Research & Book

Adair, J., (1992) Effective Leadership, 2nd Edition, Pan Books, London.

Adkins, H. and Lury, R., (1994) Gendered Work: Sexuality, Family And The Labour Market, Open University Press, Buckingham.

Aguinis, H., And Adams, S.K.R. (1998) 'Social–Role Versus Structural Models Of Gender And Influence Use In Organizations: A Strong Inference Approach'. Group And Organization Management, 23:414–446.

Aguinis, H., Nesler, M., Quigley, B.M., Lee, S.J. And Tedeschi, J.T. (1996) 'Power Bases Of Faculty Supervisors And Educational Outcomes For Graduate Students' Journal Of Higher Education, 67:267–297.

Aida, Y. And Falbo, T. (1991) 'Relationships Between Marital Satisfaction, Resources, And Power Strategies' Sex Roles, 24:43–56.

Alder, A. (1989) The Individual Psychology Of Alfred Alder: A Systematic Presentation Of Selections From His Writings, New York: Basic Books.

Alder, A. (1999) Understanding Human Nature, Translated By Colin Brett, Oxford, One World.

Aldrich. H. and Martinez, R., (2001) Entrepreneurship as Social Construction: A Multi-Level Evolutionary Approach, Penn Economic & Organizational Sociology Working Paper Abstract Series, Vol. 1 No. 3, May 2001.

Allport, G. W., (1954). The Nature of Prejudice. Cambridge, MA: Addison-Wesley.

Althusser, L., (1971) Ideology and Ideological State Apparatuses: In Lenin And Philosophy And Other Essays, London, New Left Books.

Alvesson, M., (2000) Gender and Organisation: Towards A Differentiated Understanding, Policy Studies, Open University Press.

Alvession, M. And Billing, Y.D., (1992) 'Gender and Organisation: Towards A Differentiated Understanding' Organisation Studies, 1 And 13.

Anderson, S. G., and Herr, Y. (1999) The knowledge of welfare recipients about work incentives Unpublished doctoral dissertation, University of Michigan, Ann Arbor

Argyris, C (1978) Organisational Learning: A Theory of Action Perspective, Reading, MA: Addison-Wesley.

233

Arksey, H. And Knight, P., (1999) Interviewing For Social Scientists, London: Sage.

Atkinson, R. (1998) The Life Story Interview: Quality Give Research Methods Series, 44, Sage, University Paper, London.

**B**

Ball, S. J., Bowe, R. And Gewirtz. S., (1994) Circuits Of Schooling: A Sociological Exploration Of Parental Choice Of School In Social Class Context, Sociological Review 43:1, P52-78.

Barlow, E. T., (2004) The Question Of Women In Chinese Feminism, Duke University Press, Durham And London.

Barnes, B., (1989) Managing Change: It Strategic Approach To Organizational Dynamics, London, Financial Times, Pitman Publishing.

Barrett, M., (1980) Women's Oppression Today: Problems In Marxist Feminist Analysis, London, New Left Books.

Barrett, M. And Phillips, A., (1990) Destabilising Theory: Contemporary Feminist Debates, Polity Press, Cambridge.

Basso, K. H., (1996) Wisdom Sits In Places: Notes On A Western Apache Landscape. In Steven Feld and Keith H. Basso (Eds.), Senses of Place, Santa Fe: School Of American Research Press, Pp. 53-90.

Beach, L.R., (1992) Image Theory: Decision Making In Personal and Organizational Contexts. Chichester, John Wiley & Sons.

Becker, H. S., (1970) On Methodology. In Sociological Work: Method And Substance. Chicago: Aldine Publishing Company, Pp. 3-24.

Bem, S. L. (1974). The measurement of psychological androgyny. Journal of Consulting and Clinical Psychology, 42, 155-162.

Bentler, P. M. (1992). On the fit of models to covariances and methodology to the Bulletin. Psychological Bulletin, 112, 400-404.

Bentler, P. M., & Bonett, D. G. (1980). Significance test and goodness-of-fit in the analysis of covariance structures. Psychological Bulletin, 88, 588-606.

234

Berman, A., (1998) From The New Criticism To Deconstruction: The Reception Of Structuralism And Post-Structuralism, University Of Illinois Press, Chicago.

Berg, B. (2001) Qualitative Research Methods: For The Social Sciences, 4th Edition Allyn And Bacon, Pearson Education, London

Beauvoir, S. De., (1978) The Second Sex, Tr. & Ed. By. HM Parshley. New York: Knopf.

Bourdieu, P., (1967) Systems of Education and Systems of Thought, Social Science Information, 14, P338-58.
Bourdieu, P., (1977) Cultural Reproduction and Social Reproduction, In J. Karabel And A H Hasley (Eds) Power And Ideology In Education, New York: Oxford Press.

Bourdieu, P., (1998): La Domination Masculine. Paris: Éditions De Seuil. (Collection Liber.).

Bourdieu, P., (2001) Masculine Domination, Translated By Richard Nice, Polity Press, Oxford.

Berger, J., Fisek, M.H., Norman, R.Z. And Zelditch, M., Jr. (1977) Status Characteristics And Social Interactions: An Expectation States Approach. New York, Elsevier Science.

Biernat, M. And Kobrynowicz, D., (1997) 'Gender And Race-Based Standards Of Competence: Lower Minimum Standards But Higher Ability Standards For Devalued Groups' Journal Of Personality And Social Psychology, 72:544–557.

Birkinshaw, J., (2000) Entrepreneurship In The Global Firm. Thousand Oaks: Sage.

Birrel, S., (1988) 'Discourses on the Gender /Sport Relation', Vol 16, Macmillan.

Birrell, S. (1983). The psychological dimensions of female athletic participation. In M. Boutilier & L. SanGiovanni (Eds.), The sporting woman (pp. 49-91). Champaign, IL: Human Kinetics.

Bisanz, G.L. And Rule, B.G., (1989) 'Gender And The Persuasion Schema: A Search For Cognitive Invariants'. Personality And Social Psychology Bulletin,(15:4–18.

Blackmore, J., (1993) In The Shadow Of Men: Exclusionary Theory And Discriminatory Practice In Their Historical Construction Of Masculinist Administrator Of Cultures, Gender Matters In The Theory And Practice Of Educational Administration And Policy: A Feminist Introduction, Farmer Press, London.

Blackmore, J., (1999) Troubling Women: Feminism, Leadership And Educational Change. Open University Press.

Blaikie, N. (2000) Designing Social Research, Polity Press, Oxford.

Bolton, M. And Thompson, J., (2003) Entrepreneurs In Focus: Achieve Your Potential, Thomson Learning College, London.

Bond, M. H., (1986) The Social Psychology Of A The Chinese People, M. H. Bond, The Psychology Of The Chinese People, Oxford, Oxford University Press.

Briggs, J. And Peat, F.D., (1989) Turbulent Mirror: An Illustrated Guide To Chaos Theory And The Science Of Wholeness. New York, Harper-Row.

Brooks, R., (2002). "Edinburgh, Exeter, East London – Or Employment?" A Review of Research On Young People's Higher Education Choices', Educational Research 44(2), 217-227.

Brooks, I., (2003) Organisational Behaviour: Individuals, Groups and Organisation, Second Edition, Prentice Hall, Financial Times, Essex

Brooks, A., (1997) Post-Feminism; Feminism, Cultural, Theory and Cultural Forms. Routledge.

Broverman, I.K., Vogel, S.R., Broverman, D.M., Clarkson, F.E. And Rosenkrantz, P.S., (1972) 'Sex Role Stereotypes: A Current Appraisal' Social Issues, 28:59–78.

Brown, H., (2003) Women Organizing, Routledge, London.

Browne, M. W., & Cudeck, R. (1993). Alternative ways of assessing model fit. In K. A. Bollen & J. S. Long (Eds.), Testing structural equation models (pp. 136-162). Thousand Oaks, CA: Sage.

Brown, S. L. And Eisenhardt K. M., (1997) 'The Art Of Continuous Change: Linking Complexity Theory And Time-Paced Evolution In Relentlessly Shifting Organizations' Administrative Science Quarterly, 42, 1–34.

Brown, S. L. And Eisenhardt K. M., (1998) 'Competing On The Edge: Strategy As Structured Chaos' Boston, MA: Harvard Business School Press.

236

Brustad, R. J. (1993). Who will go out and play? Parental and psychological influences on children's attraction to physical activity. Pediatric Exercise Science, 5, 210-223.

Brustad, R. J. (1996). Attraction to physical activity in urban schoolchildren: Parental socialization and gender influences. Research Quarterly for Exercise and Sport, 67, 316-323.

Burchall, D. And Lyons, L., (1995) Creating Tomorrow's Organisation; Unlocking The Benefits.

Burgoon, M., Dillard, J.P. And Doran, N.E., (1983) 'Friendly Or Unfriendly Persuasion: The Effects Of Violations By Males And Females' Human Communication Research,(10:283–294.

Butler, R., and, Blundell, K. (1995) eds. Change in Tourism: People, Places, Processes. New York: Routledge.

Butler, J., (1988): 'Performative Acts and Gender Constitution: An Essay In Phenomenology And Feminist Theory'. In: Criticism and The Theory Of The Modern Stage. P. 1097-1105. Harper.

Butler, J., (1990): Gender Trouble : Feminism And The Subversion Of Identity. New York: Routlege. (Thinking Gender. ) ISBN: 0-415-90043-3.

Butler, J., (1993): 'Imitation And Gender Insubordination'. In: The Lesbian And Gay Studies Reader. H. Abeloveet Al. (Eds.). P. 307-320. New York-London: Routledge.

Butler, J., (1993): Bodies That Matter: On The Discursive Limits Of 'Sex'. New York-London: Routledge.

Butler, J., (1997): 'Excerpt From 'Introduction' To Bodies That Matter'. In: The Gender/Sexuality Reader : Culture, History, Political Economy. R. N. Lancaster and M. Di Leonardo (Eds.). P. 531-542. Routledge.

Butler, D., and Gels, F.L., (1990) 'Nonverbal Affect Responses To Male And Female Leaders: Implications For Leadership Evaluations'. Journal Of Personality And Social Psychology, 58:48–59.

Buttner, E.H. And Mcenally, M., (1996) 'The Interactive Effect Of Influence Tactic, Applicant Gender, And Type Of Job On Hiring Recommendations' Sex Roles, 34:581–591.

Buchanan, D and Badham, R., (1999) Power, Politics and Organisational Change: Winning The Turf Game. Sage.

Byrne, D. (1998) 'Complexity Theory and The Social Sciences: An Introduction' London: Routledge.


## C

Callas M. B. And Smircich L., (1991) 'Rewriting Gender Into Organisational Theorising: Directions From Feminist Perspectives', Chapter 12 In Reed And Hughes (Eds), Rethinking Organisation: New Directions In Organisational Research And Analysis, Sage, London.

Campbell-Bradley, I., (1987) Enlightened Entrepreneurs Weidenfeld & Nicolson.

Prendergast Renee. 1991. "Cantillon and the Emergence of the Theory of Profit. "History *of Political Economy* 23: 419-29.

Capacci-Carneal, C., (2004) Community Schools In Mali: A Multilevel Analysis, The Florida State University, College Of Education, Phd

Carli, L., (1999). Gender, Interpersonal Power, and Social Influence. Journal of Social Issues, 55, 81.
Carrigan, R.W. Connell and Lee, (1985) 'Hard and Heavy: Toward A New Sociology of Masculinity,' In Beyond Patriarchy. Essays By Men On Pleasure, Power And Change, Ed. M. Kaufrnan (Toronto: Oxford University Press: 1987: 89.

Chodorow, N., (1978): The Reproduction of Mothering: Psychoanalysis and The Sociology Of Gender. Berkeley: University Of California Press. ISBN: 0520031334.

Chodorow, N., (1992): 'Heterosexuality as a Compromise Formation.' In: Psychoanalysis and Contemporary Thought, Vol. 15. Issue/No: 3. P. 267-304.

Chodorow, N., (1994): Femininities, Masculinities, Sexualities : Freud And Beyond. The University Press of Kentucky. ISBN: 0-8131-1872-7.

Chodorow, N., (1994) Gender, Revelation and Difference In Psychoanalytic Perspective. Polity Press.

Chodorow, N., (1995): 'Gender as a Personal and Cultural Construction'. In: Signs, University Of Chicago Press. Vol. 20. Issue/No: 3. P. 516-544.

Curtis C., (1998), 'Creating Culturally Responsive Curriculum: Making Race Matterthe Clearing House: A Journal Of Educational Research, Controversy And Practices17/3, P. 138.

Connell, R. W., (1985): 'Theorizing Gender.' In: Sociology, Vol. 19. Issue/No: 2. P. 260-72.

Connell, R. W., (1987): Gender and Power. Sydney: Allen & Unwin.

Connell, R. W., (1995): Masculinities. Berkeley-Los Angeles: University Of California Press.

Connell, R. W., (1996): 'Teaching the Boys: New Research on Masculinity, And Gender Strategies for Schools.' In: Teachers College Record, Vol. 2. P. 206-235.

Connell, R. W., (1997): 'Comment On Hawkesworth's 'Confounding Gender' : Re-Structuring Gender.' In: Signs: Journal of Women In Culture And Society, Vol. 22. Issue/No: 3. P. 702-707.

Connell, R.W., (1999) Masculinities. Polity Press.

Connolly, P., (1995): 'Boys Will Be Boys? Racism, Sexuality and The Construction Of Masculine Identities Amongst Infant Boys'. In: Debates and Issues in Feminist Research and Pedagogy. J. Hollandet Al. (Eds.). P. 169-195. Clevedon: The Open University Press.

Celente, G., (1990). Trend Tracking. New York: John Wiley & Sons.

Chapman, T., (1989) The Social Mobility Of Women And Men, The Social Mobility Of Women, Farmer Press, Pp 25 - 37, London

Charlesworth, K., (1997) 'A Question Of Balance? – A Survey of Managers Changing Professional and Personal Roles'. IM Research Report.

Child, J., (1999) Organisation, London, Harper and Row.

Choi, Y.B., (1993) Paradigms And Conventions: Uncertainty, Decision-Making, And Entrepreneurship. Ann Arbor, University Of Michigan Press.

Cillers, P. (1998) On Derrida and Apartheid, South Africa Journal of Philosophy, Vol. 1, Pp. 167-184.

Cillier, P., (2000) Complexity and Postmodernism: Understanding Complex Systems, Routledge, New York.

Coakley, J.J., (1994) Sport In Society – Issues And Controversies. Mosby.

Cockburn, C., (1991) In The Way Of Women: Men's Resistance To Sex Equality In Organisations, Macmillan Press, And Basingstoke.

Cockburn, C., (1998) Strategies For Gender Democracy - Strengthening The The Representation Of Trade Union Women In Their European Social Dialogue, European Journal Of Women's Studies, Vol. 3 (1), 7 – 26.

Coffey A., (1999) The Ethnographic Self: Fieldwork And The Representation Of Identity. London: Sage.

Collinson, L.D. And Hearn, J., (1996) Men As Managers; Critical Perspectives On Men, Sage.

Connell, R. (1987). Gender and power. Cambridge: Polity Press.

Coolican, H., (1990) Research Methods In Psychology. London: Hodder.

Copper Maysami, R. & Goby, V. P., (1999), "Female Business Owners In Singapore And Elsewhere: A Review Of Studies", Journal Of Small Business Management, Vol. 37, No. 2, Pp. 96-105.

Covin, J. And Miles, M., (1999) 'Corporate Entrepreneurship And The Pursuit Of Competitive Advantage, Entrepreneurship: Theory And Practice, 23:3, 47.

Craib, I., (1992) Modern Social Theory, 2nd Edn. Harvester Wheatsheaf.

Crawford, J. R., Besson, J. A. O., Bremner, M., (1992) Estimation Of Premorbid Intelligence In Schizophrenia. British Journal of Psychiatry, 161, 69-74.

Crain, R. M. (1996). The influence of age, race, and gender on child and adolescent multidimensional self-concept. In B. A. Bracken (Ed.), Handbook of self-concept; developmental, social, and clinical considerations (pp. 395-420). New York: Wiley.

Crompton, R., (1995) Women's Employment In The Middle Classes University Press.

Csizma, K. A., Wittig, A. F., & Schurr, K. T. (1988). Sport stereotypes and gender. Journal of Sport and Exercise Psychology, 10, 62-74.

Czarniawska, B., (1998) Exploring Complex Organizations: A Cultural Perspective, Second Addition, Newbury Park, Sage, California.

**D**

Daly, K. And Dienhart, A., (1998) 'Navigating The Family Domain: Qualitative Field Dilemmas' In S. Grills (Ed.) Doing Ethnographic Research: Fieldwork Settings. London: Sage.

Davidson, H. K. And Cooper, M. J., (2000) Sex Discrimination In Simulated Employment Contexts: A Meta-Analytic Investigation, Journal of Vocational Behaviour, 56, Pp 225 – 248.

Davies, L., (1990) Equity and Efficiency? School Management In An International Context. Falmer Press.

Davies, B., (1989): Frogs and Snails and Feminist Tales. Sydney: Allen and Unwin.

Davies, B., (1990): 'Agency As A Form Of Discursive Practice : A Classroom Scene Observed.' In: British Journal Of Sociology Of Education, Vol. 11. Issue/No: 3. P. 341-361.

Davies, B., (1990): 'The Problem of Desire.' In: Social Problems, Vol. 37. Issue/No: 4. P. 501-516.

Davies, B., (1991): 'The Concept of Agency: A Feminist Poststructural Analysis'. In: Social Analysis : Special Issue On Postmodern Critical Theorizing. Vol. 30. P. 42-53.

Davies, B., (1992): 'Women's Subjectivity and Feminist Stories'. In: Investigating Subjectivity. C. Ellis And M. G. Flaherty (Eds.). P. 53-76. Newbury Park, CA: SAGE.

Davies, B., (1997): 'Constructing And Deconstructing Masculinities Through Critical Literacy.' In: Gender and Education, Vol. 9. Issue/No: 1. P. 9-30.

Davies, B. And Hunt R., (1994): 'Classroom Competencies and Marginal Positionings.' In: British Journal of Sociology Of Education, Vol. 15. Issue/No: 3. P. 389-408.

Davis, C. (2004) After Poststructuralism: Reading, Stories And Theory, Routledge, London.

De Beauvoir, S. (1972): The Second Sex. Harmondsworth: Penguin.

David, M. E., (2004) Feminist Sociology and Feminist Knowledge's: Contributions To Higher Education Pedagogies And Professional Practice In The Knowledge Economy 'International Studies In The Sociology Of Education' 14 (2) P99-123.

David, M. E., (2003) Personal and Political: Feminism, Sociology and Family Lives, Stoke-On-Trent, Trentham Books.

241

David, M. E., Davies, J., Edwards, R., Reay, D. And Standing, K., (2003) 'Gender Issues In Parental Involvement In Student Choices Of Higher Education' Gender And Education 15:1, P21-23

David, M. E. and Woodward, D., (1998) Negotiating The Glass Ceiling: Careers Of Senior Women In The Academic World, Routledge Falmer London
Deal, T. And Kennedy, A., (1982) Corporate Cultures: The Rites And Rituals Of Corporate Life, M A, Addison -Wesley, Reading.

Deem, R., (2001). Globalisation New Managerialism, Academic Capitalism, And Entrepreneurialism In Universities: Is The Local Dimension Still Important? Comparative Education, 37, Pp. 7-20. February.

Delphy, C., 1984. Close To Home: A Materialist Analysis Of Women's Oppression. Amherst MA: University Of Massachusetts.

Dench, G., (1997) Transforming Men; Changing Patterns of Dependency And Dominance. Transaction Publishers.

Dennis, E. A., (Ed.). (1990). INDUSTRIAL TEACHER EDUCATION DIRECTORY. (29th Ed.). South Holland, IL: Goodheart-Willcox.

Dennis, O., (1995) "Community Development Through Indigenous Leadership." Notes On Anthropology And Intercultural Community Work 18: 30-37.

Dennis, Richard, 2001. "Inflation Expectations And The Stability Properties Of Nominal GDP Targeting," Economic Journal, Royal Economic Society, Vol. 111(468), Pages 103-13.

Denscombe, M., (1995) 'Teachers as an Audience for Research: The Acceptability of Ethnographic Approaches to Classroom Research', Teachers and Teaching: Theory and Practice, 1, 1, 173-191.

Derrida, J., (1973). Speech and Phenomena. Evanston: Northwest-Ern University Press.

Derrida, J.,(1976): Of Grammatology, Baltimore, John Hopkins University Press.

Derrida, J., (1982): Margins of Philosophy, New York/London, Harvester.

Deutschmann, D. (2000). Capitalism in crisis : globalization and world politics today. Melbourne ; New York Havana, Ocean Press ; Editora Política

Devine, C. (1999) Human Rights: The Essential Reference, ed. by H. Poole, Phoenix, Arizona: The Oryx Press.

Diamond, M. C. (1988). Enriching heredity: The impact of the environment on the anatomy of the brain. New York: Free Press.

Dickson, A., (1996) A Woman In Your Own Right. Quartet Books.

Digby T., (1998) Men Doing Feminism. Routledge, London.

Ding, Yuan-Zhu (1999). *China's Voluntary System and Activity* (Beijing, UNV).

Drake, P. And Owen, P., (1998) Gender And Management Issues In Education, An International Perspective. Trentham Books.

Drucker P., (1985) Innovation And Entrepreneurship, Practice And Principles. New York Harper & Row.

Drucker, P., (1990) 'The Emerging Theory Of Manufacturing,' Harvard Business Review, May-Jun, Pp. 94-102.

Drucker, P., (1994) Management: Tasks, Responsibilities, Practices, Butterworth Heinemann, Oxford.

Drucker, P., (Edited By Stone, N) (1998) Peter Drucker On The Profession Of Management. Harvard Business School Press With Mcgraw-Hill.

Drucker, P., (1999) 'Knowledge Worker Productivity: The Biggest Challenge,' California Management Review, 41(1) Jan, Pp. 79-94.

Drucker, P., (2000) Drucker On The Obvious And Unseen, In Chief Executive Group Magazine Vol. June 2000, Chief Executive Group, New York.

Duncan, M. C. (1994). The politics of women's body images and practices: Foucault, the panopticon, and Shape magazine. Journal of Sports and Social Issues, 18, 48-65.

**E**

Eagly, A.H., (2000). 'Social Role Theory of Sex Differences and Similarities: A Current Appraisal', In Eckes, T. And Trautner, H.M. (Eds.), The Developmental Social Psychology Of Gender. Mahwah, NJ: Erlbaum.

Eccles, J. S. (1987). Gender roles and women's achievement-related decisions. Psychology of Women Quarterly, 11, 135-172.

Eccles, J. S., & Harold, R. D. (1991). Gender differences in sport involvement: Applying the Eccles' Expectancy-Value model. Journal of Applied Sport Psychology, 3, 7-35.

Eccles, J. S., & Hoffmann, L. W. (1984). Sex roles, socialization, and occupational behaviours. In H. W. Stevenson & A. E. Siegel (Eds.), Child development research and social policy (pp. 367-420). Chicago: University of Chicago Press.

Eccles, J. S., Jacobs, J. E., & Harold, R. D. (1990). Gender role stereotypes, expectancy effects, and parent's socialization of gender differences. Journal of Social Issues, 46(2), 183-201.

Eccles, J. S., Midgley, C., & Adler, T. (1984). Grade-related changes in the school-environment: Effects on achievement motivation. In J. Nichols (Ed.), The development of achievement motivation (Vol. 3, pp. 283-331). Greenwhich, CT: JAI.

Eccles, J. S., Wigfield, A., Harold, R. D., & Blumenfeld, P. (1993). Ontogeny of children's self-perceptions and subjective task values across activity domains during the elementary school years. Child Development, 64, 830-847.

Eccles, J. S., Adler, T. F., Futterman, R., Goff, S. B., Kaczala, C. M., Meece, J., & Midgley, C. (1983). Expectancies, values and academic behaviours. In J. T. Spence (Ed.), Achievement and achievement motives (pp. 75-146). San Fransisco: Freeman.

Edwards, K. A. (1997). Troubling transformations: A collaborative inquiry into women's learning experiences in the construction and reconstruction of identities. Unpublished doctoral dissertation, University of Texas at Austin.

Edwards, B. 1999. The New Drawing on the Right Side of the Brain. Penguin Putnam, New York.

Edwards, C. and Welchman R. (1997). 'Organizational Restructuring and the Achievement of an Equal Opportunity Culture', Gender, Work and Organization, 4(1), pp. 2–12.

Eisenhardt, K., (1989). Making Fast Strategic Decisions In High Velocity Environments. Academy Of Management Journal, 32(3): 543-576.

Ely, R. J. (1995). The power in demography: Women's social constructions of gender identity at work. Academy of Management Journal, 38(3), 589-634.

**F**

Faludi, S., (1992) Backlash; The Undeclared War Crown Publishers.

244

Fasting, K. (2003). Women and sport in Norway, In I. Hartmann-Tews, & G. Pfister (Eds.), Sport and women: Social issues in international perspective (pp. 15-34). London: Routledge.

Fayol, H. 1949. General and industrial management, Paris: Dunod

Feigenbaum, M. (1978) 'Quantitative Universality For A Class Of Nonlinear Transformations' Journal Of Statistical Physics, 19:25–52. Cited In Gleick, J. P.(157.

Ferguson, K. (1984). The feminist case against bureaucracy. Philadelphia, PA: Temple University Press.

Flecher, J. K., (1999) Disappearing Acts: Gender, Power, And Relational Practice At Work, Massachusetts Institute Of Technology, MIT Press, Cambridge A.

Flanders, B. (1995, February). The information network of Kansas. Computers in Libraries,15, (2), 22-24.

Flyvbjerg, B., (2002) Mega Projects And Risks: An Anatomy Of Ambition, Cambridge University Press.

Flyvbjerg, B., (2001) [Reprinted 2002] Making Social Science Matter: Why Social Inquiry Fails And How It Can Succeed Again, Cambridge University Press, Cambridge.

Foster, David William. "Mafalda: An Argentina Comic Strip." *Journal of Popular Culture* 14 (Winter 1980): 497-508.

Foucault, M., (1968) Orders Of Discourse, Translated By Swyer, R., Social Science Information, Vol. 10. No. 2. (April, 1971), Republished As 'De Discourse On A Language' Michael Foucault, The Archaeology Of Knowledge, New York.

Foucault, M., (1977) Discipline And Punish: The Birth Of The Prison, Translated By Sheridan, A., London, Tavistock Publications.

Foucault, M., (1980) Power and Knowledge: Selected Interviews And Other Writings, 1972 - 1977, Pantheon, New York.

Foucault, M., (1981) The History Of Sexuality, Vol. 1, Harmondsworth, Penguin, London.

Foucault, M., (1986). Disciplinary Power And Subjection, Looks, Power, Blackwell, Oxford.

Foucault, M., (1979) Discipline and Punishment: The Birth of The Prison, Allen Lane, London.

Foucault, M., (1988) On Power, An Interview With Michael Foucault (1978), Reprinted In Kritzman, Foucault: Politics, Philosophy And Culture, Routledge, London.

Fox, D.J. (1969), The Research Process in Education, U.S.A., Holt, Rinehart and Winston.

Francis, B., (1999) Modernist Reductionism Or Poststructuralist Relativism: Can We Move On? An Evaluation of The Arguments In Relation To Feminist Educational Research, Gender And Education, Vol. 11, Number 4, Pp 381 – 393.

Francis, B., (2001) Boys, Girls and Achievement; Addressing The Classroom Issues, Routledge, London.

Francis, B., (2002) Relativism, Realism, And Feminism: An Analysis Of Some Theoretical Tensions In Research On Gender Identity, Journal Of Gender Studies, Volume 11, Number One, 2002.

Fredricks, J. A., & Eccles, J. S. (2002). Children's competence and value beliefs from childhood through adolescence: Growth trajectories in two male-sex-typed domains. Developmental Psychology, 38, 519-533.

Freeman, J., (2001) The Politics Of Women's Liberation, New York, And David Mcney, London.

French, J. R., and Raven B., (1959) "The Bases of Social Power." In: Studies In Social Power, Edited By Dorwin Cartwright. Ann Arbor, MI: University Of Michigan Press. Pp. 150-167.

Friedman, M., (1987) 'Beyond Caring: The De-Moralisation Of Gender' Cited In Hannen And Nelson (Eds.) 'Science And Feminist Theory' Canadian Journal Of Philosophy, No 13 (Supplement).

Fukuyama, F. (1995). Trust. New York: Free Press.

**G**

Galbraith, J. R., (2002) Strategy Implementation: Structure Systems And Process, St Paul, MN: West.

Gardiner, K. J., (2002) Masculinity Studies And Feminist Theory: New Directions, Columbia University Press, New York.

Garnaut, Ross. 2002. "Australia: A Case Study of Unilateral Trade Liberalisation." In Going Alone: The Case for Relaxed Reciprocity in Freeing Trade, edited by Jagdish Bagwati. Cambridge (MA): The MIT Press: 139–166.

Ghauri, P. And Grønhaug, K., (2002) Research Methods In Business Studies: A Practical Guide, Second Edition, Financial Times, Prentice Hall, London.

Gherardi, S. (1995). Gender, symbolism, and organizational cultures. Newbury Park, CA: Sage Publications.

Gherardi, S. (2003) Feminist Theory and Organization Theory: A Dialogue on New Bases. In Knudsen, H. and Tsoukas, H. (eds.) The Handbook of Organizational Theory: Meta-Theoretical Perspectives. Oxford: Oxford University Press.

Giddens, A., (1992): The Transformation Of Intimacy: Sexuality, Love And Eroticism In Modern Societies. Cambridge: Polity.

Giddens, A., (1994) Intimitetens Forandring: Seksualitet, Kærlighet Og Erotik I De Moderne Samfund. Copenhagen: Hans Reilzels Forlag. ISBN: 87-412-3098-1.

Giddens, A., (2001) On The Edge: Living With Global Capitalism, The Vintage Press, London.

Giddens, A., (2002) The Third Way And Its Critics, Polity Press, London.

Gill, D. L. (2002). Gender and sport behavior. In T. Horn (Ed.), Advances in sport psychology (pp. 355-375). Champaign, IL: Human Kinetics.

Glazier, J. D., (1992) Qualitative Research Methodologies For Library And Information Science: An Introduction. In Qualitative Research In Information Management, Glazier, Jack D., And Ronald R. Powell, Eds, 1-13. Englewood, Colo.: Libraries Unlimited.

Gleick, J., (1987) Chaos: Making A New Science. New York, Penguin Books.

Glover, D. And Kaplan, C., 2000. Genders. London And New York: Routledge.

Goodhall L., (1997) Take Feeding Dilemmas: Can Artificial Nutrition And Hydration Be Legally Or Ethically Withheld Or Withdrawn? Journal Of Advanced Nursing. Feb 25, 2, 217-222.

Gordon, T., (1980) Semantics: A Bibliography 1965–1978. Metuchen, NJ: Scarecrow.

247

Gramsci (1930) Antonio Gramsci. Lettere Dal Carcere. 1926-1930. 2 Vols. Ed. Antonio A. Santucci. Palermo: Sellerio Editore, 1996. International Gramsci Society Newsletter Number 6 (August, 1996): 18-22.

Grant, L., (2003) The Age Of Optimism, The Guardian, Tuesday The 27th May, Page 2 – 7.

Green, R.F., J.P. Jolly and A. Srivastava (1990), "Differentiation and Cost Leadership Strategies: A Strategic Continuum of Alternatives," Journal of Business Strategies 7(1), pp. 8 - 17.

Greendorfer, S. (1983). Shaping the female athlete: The impact of the family. In M. Boutilier & L. San Giovanni (Eds.), The sporting woman (pp. 135-155). Champaign, IL: Human Kinetics.

Gregory, E. (2003). Male gender role conflict, depression and anxiety: Clarification and generalizability to women. Journal of Counseling Psychology. 50, 167-174.

**H**

Haddon, L. (1991) 'The Cultural Production and Consumption of IT', In Mackay, H., Young, M., And Benyon, J. (Eds.) Understanding Technology In Education, Falmer Press, London.

Halford, S. And Leonard, P., (2001) Gender, Power And Organisations, Palgrave, London

Halford, S., Savage, M. And Wiltz, A., (1996) Gender, Careers And Organisations. Macmillan.)

Halfpenny, P. (1996) Conceptual history and definitions of 'Exploitation' and 'Identity' Dictionary of Sociology. London. Sage. (for 2005).

Hamel, G., (1999) Strategic Flexibility: Managing in a Turbulent Environment, Harvard Press.

Hamersley, M. And Akinson, P., (1998) Ethnography: Principles And Practice, 2nd Edition, Routledge, London.

Hansard Commission (1990) http://www.hansardsociety.org.uk/

Haraway, D., J., How Like a Leaf, Donna J. Haraway: An interview with Thyrza Nichols Goodeve. Routledge. New York, Harding, S (1986) *The Science Question in Feminism*. Milton Keynes: Open University Press.

248

Hargreaves, A., (1997) 'Restructuring Restructuring: Postmodernity And The Prospects For Educational Change', Unpublished Paper, Ontario Institute For Studies In Education.

Hargreaves, J., (1986) Sport, Power And Culture; A Social And Historical Analysis Of Popular Sports In Britain. St Martin's.

Hargreaves, J., (1994) Sporting Females, Critical Issues In The History And Sociology Of Woman's Sport. Routledge).

Harriman Helga H., (1995) Women--History Of--Western Civilization Conneticut : The Dushkin Publishing Group.

Harrison, D. A., Price, K. H. And Bell M. P., (1998) 1998 "Beyond Relational Demography: Time And The Effects Of Surface- And Deep-Level Diversity On Work Group Cohesion." Academy Of Management Journal, 41: 95-107.

Harrison, D. A., Price, K. H., Gavin, J. H., And Florey, A. T., (2002). Time, Teams, And Task Performance: Changing Effects Of Surface- And Deep-Level Diversity On Group Functioning. Academy Of Management Journal, 45: 1029-1045.

Hartmann-Tews, I., & Pfister, G. (2003). Women's inclusion in sport: International and comparative findings. In I. Hartmann-Tews & G. Pfister (Eds.), Sport and women: Social issues in international perspective (pp. 266-280). London: Routledge.

Hassard, J., (2002) 'Organizational Time: Modern, Symbolic And Postmodern Reflections', Organisation Studies, 23: 885-892.

Hassard, J. P., Eds (1993): Postmodernism And Organizations. Sage Publications, London-Newbury Park-New Delhi.

Hassard, J., (2002) 'Organizational Time: Modern, Symbolic And Postmodern Reflections', Organisation Studies, 23: 885-892.

Hattie, J. (1992). Self-concept. Hillsdale, NJ: Erlbaum.

Hayes, S. D., Crocker, P. R. E., & Kowalski, K. C. (1999). Gender differences in physical self-perceptions, global self-esteem, and physical activity: Evaluation of the physical self-perception profile model. Journal of Sport Behaviour, 22, 1-14.

He, Xue-Zhong., 2001. "Dynamics Of Beliefs And Learning Under AI Processes - The Homogeneous Case," Research Paper Series 53, Quantitative Finance Research Centre, University Of Technology, Sydney.

He, T., (2002) "An Adaptive Model On Asset Pricing And Wealth Dynamics With Heterogeneous Trading Strategies," Computing In Economics And Finance 2002 135, Society For Computational Economics.

Healey, M., Robinson, G., & Castleford, J., (1994). Innovation In Geography Teaching In Higher Education: Developing The Potential For Computer-Assisted Learning. In 28th International Geographical Congress, Commission On Geographical Education, Innovation In Geographical Education: Proceedings (Pp. 199-203) Amsterdam: Centrum Voor Educatieve Geografie Vrije Universiteit.

Hearn, J., (1996): 'Is Masculinity Dead? A Critique Of The Concept Of Masculinity/Masculinities'. In: Understanding Masculinities. M. Mac An Ghaill (Ed.). P. 202-217. Buckingham: Open University Press.

Hearn, J., (1996): The Implications Of Critical Studies On Men. School Of Social Policy, University Of Manchester.

Hearn, J. And Parkin, P. W., (1992) Organisational Theory, Modern, Symbolic And Post-Modern Perspectives, Oxford University Press, Oxford.

Hearn, J. And Parkin, W., (2001) Gender, Sexuality And Violence In Organisations, Sage Publications, London.

Heene, A. And Sanchez, R., (1997) Competence-Based Strategic V Management, Chichester, John Wiley & Sons.

Hennig, J. And Jardim, R., [1977] (2003) The Managerial Woman, Garden City, New York.

Henry, J., (2001) Creativity and Perception In Management, Open University, Sage Publication, London.

Herricks, E. E., "An Ecological Design Paradigm For Watershed Management," International Workshop On Watershed Management In The 21st Century, May 30-31, 2000, Taipei, Taiwan. Pp. 73-93 (2000).

Hertz, E., (1997) The Trading Crowd: An Ethnography Of The Shanghai Stock Market, Cambridge University Press, Cambridge.

Hill, R.C. And Levenhagen, M., (1995) 'Metaphors and Mental Models: Sense Making And Sensegiving In Innovative And Entrepreneurial Activities.' Journal of Management, (21(6):1057–1074.)

Hodge, D. R., (2001). Spiritual Assessment: A Review of Major Qualitative Methods and A New Framework For Assessing Spirituality. Social Work, 46(3), 203-214.

Hogg, M. A., (2005). Uncertainty, Social Identity and Ideology. In S. R. Thye & E. J. Lawler (Eds.), Advances In Group Processes (Vol. 22, Pp. 203-230). New York: Elsevier.

Holland, J. (1993): Sexuality And Ethnicity: Variations In Young Women's Sexual Knowledge And Practice. London: The Tufnell Press. (WRAP Paper (Women Risk AIDS Project). No. 8.) ISBN: 1872767850.

Holland, J. And Ramazanoglu, C., (1993): 'Women's Sexuality and Men's Appropriation Of Desire'. In: Up Against Foucault: Explorations Of Some Tensions Between Foucault And Feminism. C. Ramazanoglu (Ed.). London: Routledge.

Holland, J., (1991): Learning About Sex: Young Women And The Social Construction Of Sexual Identity. London: The Tufnell Press. (WRAP Paper (Women Risk AIDS Project). No. 4.)

Holland, J., (1992): Pressured Pleasure: Young Women And The Negotiation Of Sexual Boundaries. London: The Tufnell Press. (WRAP Paper (Women Risk AIDS Project). ) ISBN: 187276780x.

Holland, J., (1994): 'Desire, Risk And Control: The Body As A Site Of Contestation'. In: AIDS : Setting A Feminist Agenda. L. Doyalet Al. (Eds.). P. 61-79. London: Taylor & Francis.

Holland, J., And M. Blair (1995): Debates And Issues In Feminist Research And Pedagogy. Clevedon-Philadelphia: The Open University/Multi-Lingual Matters. ISBN: 1853592528.

Holland, J., (1991): Pressure, Resistance, Empowerment : Young Women And The Negotiation Of Safer Sex. London: The Tufnell Press. (WRAP Paper (Women Risk AIDS Project). No. 6.) ISBN: 1-872767-75-3.

Holland, J., (1992): 'Risk, Power And The Possibility Of Pleasure: Young Women And Safer Sex.' In: AIDS Care, Vol. 4. Issue/No: 3. P. 273 - 283.

Holland, J., (1993): Wimp Or Gladiator: Contradictions In Acquiring Masculine Sexuality. London: Tufnell Press.

Holland, J., (1994): 'Power And Desire: The Embodiment Of Female Sexuality.' In: Feminist Review, Vol. 46. P. 21-38.

Holland, J., (1998): The Male In The Head: Young People, Heterosexuality And Power. London: The Tufnell Press.

Holland, J., Ramazanoglu, C., Sharp, S. And Thomson, R. (2004) The Male In The Head: Young People, Heterosexuality And Power, Tufnell Press London.

Holland, J.H., (1998) Emergence From Chaos To Order, Oxford University Press, Oxford.

Holloway, W. And Jefferson, T., (2004) Doing Qualitative Research Differently: Free Association, Narrative And The Interview Method, Sage Publications, London.

Holloway, W., (1983): 'Heterosexual Sex : Power And Desire For The Other'. In: Sex And Love: New Thoughts On Old Contradictions. S. Cartledge And J. Ryan (Eds.). London: Women's Press.

Hooks B., (1989) Talking Back: Thinking Feminist, Thinking Black Sheba, London.

Horn, T. S. (1987). The influence of teacher-coach behavior on the psychological development of children. In D. Gould & M. R. Weiss (Eds.), Advances in pediatric sport sciences. Vol. 2: Behavioral issues (pp. 121-142). Champaign. IL: Human Kinetics.

Houston, A. C. (1983). Sex-typing. In P. Mussen & E. M. Heteringhton (Eds.), Handbook of child psychology (Vol. IV, pp. 387-467). New York: Wiley.

Hu, L., & Bentler, P. M. (1995). Evaluating model fit. In R. H. Hoyle (Ed.), Structural equation modelling: Concepts, issues, and applications (pp. 76-99). London: Sage.

Hübler, A., (1992) 'Modelling And Control Of Complex Systems: Paradigms And Applications' In Lam, L. (Ed.) Modeling Complex Phenomena. New York, Springer. Hutheesing (1990).

I

IIM (2003) National Management Salary Survey, Institute Of Management (In Association With Remunerations Economics) Kingston Upon Thames.

Irvine, M., (1998) Global Cyberculture Reconsidered: Cyberspace, Identity, And The Global Informational City, Paper Orginally Delivered At INET '98, Geneva. Revised 10.17.99.

J

Jackson, N. And Carter, P., (2000) 'Rethinking Organisational Behaviour' Financial Times, Prentice Hall.

Jacobs, J. E., Lanza, S., Osgood, D. W., Eccles, J. S., & Wigfield, A. (2002). Changes in children's self-competence and values: Gender and domain differences across grades 1 through 12. Child Development, 73, 509-527.

James M., (1986), Strategic Database Design, Englewood Cliffs, New Jersey, Prentice Hall.

Jankowicz, W., (2001) Romantic Passion In The People's Republic Of China, Columbia University Press, New York.

Jefferson, T., (2003) 'Muscle, 'Hard Men' And 'Iron' Mike Tyson: Reflections On Desire, Anxiety And The Embodiment Of Masculinity, Body And Society, 4 (1): 77-98.

Johnson. L., (1992) Agents That Learn To Explain Themselves. In Proceedings Of The National Conference On Artificial Intelligence, Pages 1257-1263, Seattle, WA, August 1994. AAAI, AAAI Press.

Jones, S., (2002). The Internet Goes To College. Retrieved September 20, 2002, From Http://Www.Pewinternet.Org/.

Joreskog, K. G., & Sorbom, D. (1993). LISREL 8: Structural equation modeling with the SIMPLIS command language. Chicago: Scientific Software International.

Joreskog, K. H., & Sorbom, D. (1999). LISREL 8: Structural equation modeling with the SIMPLIS command language. Chicago: Scientific Software International.

**K**

Kane, M. J., & Snyder, E. (1989). Sport typing: The social "containment" of women. Arena Review, 13, 77-96.

Kanter, R. M. (1977) Men and Women Of The Corporation: Basic Books, New York

Kanter, R. M. (1977/93) The Change Masters, Simon And Schuster, New York.

Kanter (1997) Men and Women of The Corporation, Second Edition, Basic Books, New York

Kanuha, V. K. (2000). "Being Native" Versus "Going Native": Conducting Research As An Insider. Social Work, 45(5), 439–447.

Kaple. D. A., 1995. "Voices From The Underground", Mimeo Kaufmann, M. (1999) Beyond Patriarchy: Essays By Men On Pleasure, Power, And Change, Oxford University Press Toronto.

Kelly, R. M. (2004) Their Gendered Economy: Work, Careers and Success, Second Ed Sage, London.

Kelly, R. M. & Lahti, G. (2000) The Study Of Gender Power And Its Link To Governance And Leadership. In Duerst-Lahti, Georgia & Kelly, Rita Mae (eds.)

Kelsey, D. 2002. "U.S. Women's Net Use Grows At Triple The Rate Of Men's." In Washington Post. Washington, D.C

Kiesling (2001) Politeness, Humor And Gender In The Workplace: Negotiating Norms And Identifying Contestation Volume: 1 Issue: 1 Page(S): 121-149

Kirk, Jerome And Marc Miller. 1986. Reliability And Validity In Qualitative Research. Newbury Park:Sage Publications.

Kirzner, I.(1973) Competition And Entrepreneurship. Chicago: University Of Chicago Press. Klomsten, A. T., Skaalvik, E. M., & Espnes, G. A. (2004). Physical self-concept and sports: Do gender differences still exist? Sex Roles, 50, 119-127.

Koivula, N. (1995). Ratings of gender appropriateness of sports participation: Effects of gender-based schematic processing. Sex Roles, 33, 543-557.

Koivula, N. (2001). Perceived characteristics of sports categorized as gender-neutral, feminine, and masculine. Journal of Sport Behaviour, 24, 377-393.

Kristeva (1977) "A New Type Of Intellectual: The Dissident," In The Kristeva Reader, Edited By Toril Moi, New York: Columbia University Press, 1986; Originally Published In 1977.

Kristeva (1981) Powers Of Horror, Trans. By Leon Roudiez, New York: Columbia University Press, 1982.

Kristeva (1984) "Julia Kristeva In Conversation With Rosiland Coward," Desire, ICA Documents, 1984, P. 22-27

Kristeva, Julia, 1986, Women's Time, In The Kristeva Reader, Toril Moi (Ed.). New York: Columbia University Press,. 187–213.

Kuhn, S. E. "How Business Helps Schools." Fortune 121, No. 12 (Spring 1990): 91-94.

Kumar, K. (1995) Post-Industrial To Post-Modern Society. New Theories Of The Contemporary World, UK, Blackwell.

Knights, D. And Willmott, H. (2000) Management Lives: Power And Identity In Work Organisations, Sage, London.

**L**

Lacan, Jacques (1977) The Four Fundamental Concepts Of Psychoanalysis. London: Hogarth.

Lakoff, G. And Johnson, M. (1995) Metaphors We Live By. Chicago, IL, University Of Chicago Press.)

Lee, E. W. Y. (2003) Gender And Change In Hong Kong: Globalization, Post Colonialism, And Chinese Patriarchy, University Of British Columbia, UBC Press, Canada.

Leinbach, T. R. (1997) "Development And Liberalization: The Airline Industry In ASEAN." In G. C. Hufbauer And C. Findlay, Eds., Flying High. Liberalizing Civil Aviation In The Asia Pacific. Institute For International Economics, Washington, D.C.

Leithwood, K., "The Move Towards Transformational Leadership". Educational Leadership, Vol.49, No.5, 1992, 8-12.

Leithwood, K., "Leadership For School Restructuring". Educational Administration Quarterly, 30, 4, 1994, 498-518.

Leithwood, K And Tomlinson, D And Genge, M., "Transformational School Leadership" In Leithwood, K. (Ed)., International Handbook On Educational Leadership. Kluwer, Norwall, MA, 1996.

Lewin, R. (2001) Complexity: Life At The Edge Of Chaos, Second Edition, Phoenix Paperback, London.

Lingard, B. And Douglas, P. (1999) Men Engaging Feminisms: Pro-Feminism, Backlashes And Schooling, Open University Press.

Lingard, B., Hayes, D., Mills, M. And Christie, P. (2003) Leading Learning: Making Hope Practical In Schools. Buckingham, Open University Press.

Lingard, B. And Douglas, P. (1999) Men Engaging Feminisms: Profeminism, Backlashes And Schooling. Buckingham,Open University Press.

Lingard, B. (2000) It Is And It Isn't: Vernacular Globalisation, Educational Policy And Restructuring. In Burbules, N. And Torres, C. (Eds) Globalisation And Education. New York, Routledge, Pp. 79-108.

Lingard, B. (2003) Where To In Gender Policy In Education After Recuperative Masculinity Politics? International Journal Of Inclusive Education, 7 (1), Pp.33-56.

Lingard, B. (2001) Some Lessons For Educational Researchers: Repositioning Research In Education And Education In Research. Australian Educational Researcher. 28 (3), Pp.1-46.

Lingard, B., Hayes, D. And Mills, M. (2003) Teachers And Productive Pedagogies: Contextualising, Conceptualising, Utilising. Pedagogy, Culture And Society, 11 (3), Pp.399-424.

Lingard, B. And Rawolle, S. (2004) Mediatizing Educational Policy: The Journalistic Field, Science Policy, And Cross-Field Effects, Journal Of Education Policy, 19 (3), Pp.361-380.

Lipman-Blumen, J, And Drucker, P (2000) Connective Leadership: Managing In A Changing World. Oxford University Press.

Lips, H. M. (1994) 'Female Power: A Case Of Cultural Preparedness', In H. L. Radtke And H. J. Stam (Eds), Power And Gender: Social Relations In Theory And Practice, Pp. 89-107, Sage, London.

Liu, B. And P. Link (1998). "A Great Leap Backward ?" The New York Review Of Books XLV, N° 15 (October 8): Pp. 19 - 23

Loden, M. (1985). Feminine Leadership Or How To Succeed In Business Without Being One Of The Boys. New York: Times Books.

Lu Xun (1995) Bibliography Of Bruce Lee, Hong Kong

Lukes, S. (1974). Power: A Radical View. New York: Routledge

**M**

Macrae, N. 1976. The Coming Entrepreneurial Revolution: A Survey. The Economist, December 25.

Malinowski, Bronislaw. 1935. Coral Gardens And Their Magic. London: Allen & Unwin. - 1922. Argonauts Of The Western Pacific. London: G. Routledge.

256

Mandelbrot, B. (1977) The Fractal Geometry Of Nature. New York, Freeman.

Manolova, T.S., Brush, C.G., Edelman, L.F. And Greene, P.G., 2002, Internationalization Of Small Firms: Personal Factors Revisited. International Small Business Journal 20 (1), 9-31.

March, J. G., And Simon, H. A., 1993 [1958]. Organizations. 2nd Ed. London: Blackwell Marlow (2002).

Marsh, H. W. (1989). Age and sex effects in multiple dimensions of self-concept: Preadolescence to early-childhood. Journal of Educational Psychology, 81, 417-430.

Marsh, H. W. (1996a). Construct validity of Physical Self-Description Questionnaire responses. Relations to external criteria. Journal of Sport and Exercise Psychology, 18(2), 111-131.

Marsh, H. W. (1996b). Physical self description questionnaire: Stability and discriminant validity. Research Quarterly for Exercise and Sport, 67, 249-264.

Marsh, H. W. (1997). The measurement of physical self-concept: A construct validation approach. In K, Fox (Ed.), The physical self-concept: From motivation to well-being (pp. 27-58). Champaign, IL: Human Kinetics.

Marsh, H. W., & Redmayne, R. S. (1994). A multidimensional physical self-concept and its relation to multiple components of physical fitness. Journal of Sport & Exercise Psychology, 16, 45-55.

Marsh, H. W., Richards, G. E., Johnson, S., Roche, L., & Tremayne, P. (1994). Physical Self Description Questionnaire: Psychometric properties and a multitrait-multimethod analysis of relations to existing instruments. Journal of Sport & Exercise Psychology, 16, 270-305.

Marshall, W. L., Anderson, D., & Fernandez, Y. (Eds.). (1999). Cognitive Behavioural Treatment Of Sexual Offenders. New York: John Wiley & Sons.

Marshall, W. L., & Fernandez, Y. M. (2000). Phallometric Testing With Sexual Offenders: Limits To Its Value. Clinical Psychology Review, 20, 807-822.

Martino, W., Lingard, B. And Mills, M. (2004) Issues In Boys' Education: A Question Of Teacher Threshold Knowledges?, Gender And Education, 16 (4), Pp.435-454.

Matteo, S. (1986). The effects of sex and gender-schematic processing on sport participation. Sex Roles, 15, 417-432.

Matteo, S. (1988). The effect of gender-schematic processing on decisions about sex inappropriate sport behaviour. Sex Roles, 18, 41-58.

Mills, M., Martino, W. And Lingard, B. (2004) Attracting, Recruiting And Retaining Male Teachers: Policy Issues In The Male Teacher Debate, British Journal Of Sociology Of Education, 25 (3), Pp.355-369.

May, T. ( 1999 ) Situating Social Theory, Buckingham, Open University Press, UK.

May, T. ( 2001 ) Social Research: Issues And The Methods, Open University Press, UK.

Mayers C K, An Investigation Of The Implications And Effectiveness Of Producer Responsibility For The Disposal Of WEEE (Engd Thesis). 2002, Brunel: Guildford.

Mccracken, G. (1988) The Long Interview: Qualitative Research Methods Series, 13, Sage, University Paper, London.

Mcdowell, L. (1999) Gender, Identity And Place: Understanding Feminist Geographies, Polity Press, Cambridge.

Mcnay, L. (1992) Foucault And Feminism: Power, Gender And The Self, North-Eastern University Press, Boston.

Mcnay, L. ( 2000 ) Gender And Agency, Cambridge, Polity Press.

Mcgrath. C., J. (2001). "Toward Improving Female Retention In The Computer Science Major." Communications Of The ACM. Published May, 2001 Mellon (1990)

Mendell, A. (1996) How Men Think: The Seven Essential Rules For Making It In A Man's World. New York And Toronto, Random House.

Messner, M. A. (1988). Sports and male domination: The female athlete as contested ideological terrain. Sociology of Sport Journal, 5, 197-211.

Messner, M. A. (1990). Men studying masculinity: Some epistemological issues in sport sociology. Sociology and Sport Journal, 7, 136-153.

Messner, M. A., Duncan, M. C., & Jensen, K. (1993). Separating the men from the girls: The gendered language of televised sports. Gender & Society, 7, 121-137.

Metheny, E. (1965). Symbolic forms of movement: The feminine image in sports. In E. Metheny (Ed.), Connotations of movement in sport and dance (pp. 43-56). Dubuque, IA: Brown.

Miles, M.B. And Huberman A.M. 1994 Qualitative Data Analysis 2 Nded. Thousand Oaks, California: Sage.

Miller, J. (1991). The Construction Of Anger In Women And Men. In J. Jordan, A. Kaplan, J. Miller, I. Stiver & 1. Surrey. (Eds.), Women's Growth In Connection (Pp. 181-198). New York: Guilford.

Mills, A. J. (1992) Organisation, And Gender And Culture, Sage, London.

Mills, S. (Ed.) 1994. Gendering The Reader. Hemel Hempstead: Harvester Wheatsheaf.

Mills, S. (1995) 'Become The Man That Women Desire': Gender Identities And Dominant Discourses...Mullany Language And Literature.2004; 13: 291-305.

Mills, A. (2002). ' Studying The Gendering Of Organisational Culture Over Time: Concerns, Issues And Strategies' Gender, Work And Organization 9 (3): 286-307.

Mills, J.A. And Tancred, P. (1995) Gendering Organisational Analysis. Sage.

Mintzberg, H. (2002). Beyond Selfishness. MIT Sloan Management Review, 67-74, Fall.

Mintzberg, H. (2004). Managers Not MBA's. London: Pearson Education.

Morgan, G. (1986) Images Of The Organization. Newbury Park, CA, Sage.

Morgan, G. (1996) Images Of The Organization. Second Edition Newbury Park, CA, Sage.

Movius, B. (2004) Weathers Permitting, Baton Rouge & London: Louisiana State Univ. Press, April, 2005.

Mulgan, G. And Worpole, K. (1986) Saturday Night or Sunday Morning, Comedia, London

Mulholland, K. (1996) Entrepreneurialism, Masculinities and The Self-Made Man: In Men As Managers, Managers As Men: Critical Perspectives On Men, Masculinities And Managements, Edited By Collinson, D. And Hearn, J. London: Sage.

Myer (1995) Narrow - Management/Leadership, Prentice Hall, London.

**N**

National Foundation For Women Business Owners, Key Issues Affecting Women Business Owners In Argentina And Other Latin And Iber-American Countries, April (1998/2003). British Journal Of Management, Chichester: Mar 1998, Vol. 9, Iss. 1; Pg. 41, 11 Pgs.

Neuhauser, P. Bender, R. And Stromberg, K. (2000) Culture.Com: Building Corporate Culture, Wiley, 2000.

Nicholson, P. (1996) Gender, Power And Organisation: A Psychological Perspective, Routledge, London.

NOLAN, B. 2002. "Earnings Inequality, Returns To Education And Immigration Into Ireland", Labour Economics, Vol. 9, No. 5.

## O

Oakley, A. (1997): The Gendering Of Methodology : An Experiment In Knowing. Uppsala: The Swedish Collegium For Advanced Study In The Social Sciences. (Seminar For SCASSS. )

Oglesby, E. 2001. "Machos And Machetes In Guatemala's Cane Fields." In NACLA Report On The Americas 34: 16–17

Onwuegbuzie, A. J. (2002). Positivists, Post-Positivists, Post-Structuralists, And Post- Modernists: Why Can't We All Get Along? Towards A Framework For Unifying Research Paradigms. Education, 122 (3), 518-530.

Ostrow, A. C. (1981). Age grading: Implications for physical activity participation among older adults. Quest, 33, 112-123.

Ostrow, A. C., Jones, D. C., & Spiker, D. A. (1981). Age role expectations and sex role expectations for selected sport activities. Research Quarterly for Exercise and Sport, 52, 216-227.

Owen, J. (2002) Management Stripped Bare: What They Don't Teach You At Business School, Coogan Page, London.

Ozga, J. (Ed.) (1993) Women In Educational Management, Open University Press, Buckingham.

## P

Pacanowsky, M., O'Donnel-Trujillo, N. (1983). "Organizational Communication As Cultural Performance." Communication Monographs, Vol. 50, Pp. 126-147.

Pascale (2002) Surfing Of The Edge Of Chaos, Prentice Hall, London.

Pedersen, D. M., & Kono, D. M. (1990). Perceived effects on femininity of the participation of women in sport. Perceptual and Motor Skills, 71, 783-792.

Peters, T. And Waterman, P. (1982) In Search Of Excellence, Penguin, New York.

Pfister, G. (1993). Appropriation of the environment, motor experiences and sporting activities of girls and women. International Review for the Sociology of Sport, 28, 159-171.

Pfister, G. (2000). Women and the Olympic Games. In B. L. Drinkwater (Ed.), Women in sport (pp. 3-19). Oxford: Blackwell Science.

Pfister, G., & von der Lippe, G. (1994). Women's participation in sports and the olympic games in Germany and Norway: A sociohistorical analysis. Journal of Comparative Physical Education and Sport, 16, 30-41.

Pinchot, G. (1985). Intrapreneuring. New York, NY: Harper And Row.

Poggenpoel (2001) RESEARCHER AS RESEARCH INSTRUMENT IN EDUCATIONAL RESEARCH: A POSSIBLE THREAT TO TRUSTWORTHINESS? Education, Vol. 100. Faculty Of Education And Nursing Rand Afrikaans University.

Poggenpoel, M,. Myburgh, C, & Van Der Linde. C. 2001, 'Qualitative Research Strategies As Prerequisites For Quantitative Strategies,' Education, Vol. 122. Pp. 408-414.

Powell, N.G. (1993) Women And Men In Management. Sage, Newbury Park, California.

**R**

Rabinow, P. (1991) The Foucault Reader: An Introduction To Foucault's Thought, Penguin Books, New York.

Rabinow, P. (1998) Power And Knowledge: Selected Interviews And Other Writings 1972 -1977, Edited By Colin Gordon, Harvester Press Ltd, London.

Reed, M. (1996) The Sociology Of Management, Second Edition, Harvest Wheatsheaf, London.

Reid-Yarnell, R., (1999) The New Entrepreneur, Addicus Books London

Reinharz, S. (1992). Feminist Methods In Social Research. New York: Oxford University Press, Inc.

Ribbens, J. And Edwards, R. (1998) Feminist Dilemmas In Qualitative Research: Public Knowledge And Private Lives, London: Sage

Richardson, G.P. (1991) Feedback Thought In The Social Sciences And Systems Theory. University Press.

Robins, S. P. (1984) Essentials Of Organisational Behaviour, Third Edition, Prentice-Hall, New Jersey.

Robinson, James C. (1984). "Racial Inequality And The Probability Of Occupation-Related Injury Or Illness," Milbank Memorial Fund Quarterly 62, 567–590.

Russell, B. (1996) Power, Routledge Classics, 2004, Cornwall.

Robson, C. (1993). Real World Research: A Resource For Social Scientists And Practitioner-Researchers. Oxford: Blackwell.

Rolston Homes (1995) Human Values And Natural Systems: Society And Natural Resources 35 (4), 374-386.

Rosenau, P. (1992) Post-Modernism And The Social Sciences. Princeton, NJ, Princeton University Press.

Rosenberg J., (1997) "The Interactive Diagram Sentence: Hypertext as a Medium of Thought" in Visible Language, 30(2), 103-116, 1997.

Reay, D. , David, M. And Ball, S. (2005) Degrees Of Choice: Social Class, Race And Gender In Higher Education Trentham Books.

S

State Development Research Centre (2003) Almanac Of China's Economy, Beijing, Publishing House.

Sarup, M. (1993) An Introductory Guide To Poststructuralism And Post-Modernism, Second Edition, Georgia, Athens.

Sattel, Jack. 1983. "Men, Inexpressiveness, And Power." In Language, Gender And So-Ciety, Ed. Barrie Thorne, Cheris Kramarae, And Nancy Henley, 119–24. Rowley, Mass.: Newbury.

Saunders, C. S. (1998) There Strategic Contingencies Theory Of Power: Multiple Perspectives, Journal Of Management Studies, Vol. 27, Pp 1 – 18.

Saunders, I. (2001) Strategic Thinking And Their New Science: Planning In The Midst Of Chaos, Complexity, And Change, A Free Press, New York.

Saunders, M., Lewis, P. And Thornhill, A. (1997) Research Methods For Business Students, Financial Times, Pitman Publishing.

Saunders, M., Lewis, P. And Thornhill, A. (1997) Research Methods For Business Students, Third Edition, Financial Times, Pitman Publishing.

Saussure, Ferdinand de [1915] (1966) Course In General Linguistics. New York: McGraw-Hill.

Savage, M. & Witz, A. (eds.) (1992) Gender And Bureaucracy. Oxford: Blackwell/The Sociological Review.

Savage, M., B. James, P. Dickens, T. Fielding (1995) Property Bureaucrasy And Culture : Middle Class Formation In Contemporary Britain, Routledge, London, N.Y.

Sax J. L. (1968) Water Laws Planning And Policies, Cases And Materials Contemporary  Legal Education Services, The Bobbs Meril Inc. New York .

Schein, V.E., 1976, 'Think manager - Think Male', The Atlanta Economic Review, March/April, pp.21-24.
Schlossberg, M. (2004). Is Sprawl Unhealthy? A Multi-Level Analysis Of The Relationship Of Metropolitan Sprawl To The Health Of Individuals, Journal Of Planning Education And Research 24: 184-196.

Schumpeter J. A. (1934) The Theory Of Economic Development, Cambridge, MA, Harvard University Press.

Scott. C., (1989). "Household Labor And The Routine Production Of Gender." Social Problems 36: 473-490.

Scott J. (2002). "Time-Dependent Effects Of Wives' Employment On Marital Dissolution." American Sociological Review, 66, 2 (April): 226-245.

Scratton, S (1992) Shaping up to Womanhood: Gender and Girls' Physical Education. Milton Keynes: Open University Press.

Searle, R. J. (1995) The Construction Of Social Reality, Penguin Books, London.

Sedgwick, E. K. (2000) Between Men: English Literature And Male Homiosocial Desire, Columbia University Press, New York.

Senge, P.M. (1992) The Fifth Discipline. Century Business.

Shaw, J. (2001) 'European Union Governance And The Question Of Gender: A Critical Comment'. Responses To The European Commission's White Paper On Governance – Jean Monnet Papers. Available At: Http://Www.Jeanmonnetprogram.Org/01/010601.Html.

Shelton, Anthony. 2001. Unsettling The Meaning: Critical Museology, Art And Anthropological Discourses. In Academic Anthropology And The Museum Christine M. S., 2001 "Women On Power: Leadership Redefined," Edited By Freeman, And Bourque, Northeastern University Press. Chapter, "Leadership, Sport, And Gender," By Tucker Center Director, Mary Jo Kane.Shenkar And Ronen.

Shijin Yoo (2004), "Essays On Customer Equity And Product Marketing," Doctoral Dissertation, UCLA Anderson School Of Management.42 Shilton (2001).

Silverman, D. (1997) Qualitative Research: Theory, Method And Practice, Sage Publications, London.

Silverman, D. (1998) Harvey Sacks: Social Science And Conversational Analysis, Cambridge Polity, Oxford University Press, New York.

Silverman, D. (2004) Interpreting And Qualitative Data: Methods For Analysing Talk, Text And Interaction, Second Edition, Sage Publications, London.

Sinclair, A. (2000) Teaching Managers About Masculinities: Are You Kidding?, Management Learning, 31, One, Pp 83 - 101.

Skinner, B.F. (1954). The Science Of Learning And The Art Of Teaching. Harvard Educational Review, 24(2), 86-97.

Smircich, L. (1981). The Concept Of Culture And Organizational Analysis. Paper Presented At The SCA/ICA Conference On Interpretive Approaches To Organizational Communication. Alta, UT.

Smith B. (1982), 'Racism And Women's Studies' From G Hull, P Scott & B Smith (Eds) All The Women Are White, All The Blacks Are Men, But Some Of Us Are Brave Feminist Press, New York.

Smith, D. E. (1990) The Conceptual Practices Of Power, A Feminist Sociology Of Knowledge. Boston: Northeastern University Press.

264

Snyder, E. E., & Spreitzer, E. (1983). Change and variation in social acceptance of female participation. Journal of Sport Behavior, 6, 3-8.

Stacey, R. (1996) Complexity And Creativity In Organizations. San Francisco, CA, Berrett Koehler.).

Stacey, R. And Griffin, J. D. (2000) Complexity And Management: Fad Or Radical Challenge To Systems Thinking?, London Routledge.

Stacey, R. (2001) Complex Responsive Processes In Organisations: Learning And Knowledge Creation, London: Routledge.

Stacey, R. (2003) Strategic Management And Organisational Dynamics: The Challenge Of Complexity, 4th Edition, Prentice Hall, Financial Times.

Streatfield, J. P. ( 2002) The Paradox Of Control In Organisations, Routledge, London.

Stivers, C. (1992) Gender Images In Public Administration: Legitimacy And The Administrative State Thousand Oaks, CA: Sage Publications

Strati, A. (1992). Aesthetic Understanding Of Organizational Life. Academy Of Management Review, 17(3), 568-581.

Strauss, A. And Corbin, J. (1990) Basics Of Qualitative Research: Grounded Theory Procedures And Techniques. Newbury Park: Sage.

Sung, J. (1996). Factors Related To Household Risk Tolerance: An Ordered Probit Analysis. Proceedings Of The 42nd Annual Conference Of The American Council On Consumer Interests, 221-228.

Swaffar, J. K. (2002) "Heroes And Reunification: The Resistance Of Cultural Memory From Two Germanies." Heroes And Heroism In German Culture.Stephen Brockmann And James Steakley, Eds. Amsterdan: Rodopi, 2001. 131-156.

## T

Tajfel, H. (1981). Human Groups And Social Categories. Cambridge, England: Cambridge University Press.

Talbot M. (1988) Understanding The Relationships Between Women And Sport: The Contribution Of British Feminist Approaches In Leisure And Cultural Studies International Review For The Sociology Of Sport 23. 1.

Tannen, D. 1990. You Just Don't Understand: Women And Men In Conversation. New York: Ballantine Books.

Tannen, D. (2001) Women And Men At Work: Language, Sex And Power, Talking From 9 To 5, Psychology Business, Oxford University Press, London.

Tanton, M. (Ed.). (1994). Women In Management: A Developing Presence. New York: Routledge.

Taylor C (1975), Hegel (Cambridge, USA: Cambridge University Press.

Taylor, B.H., 1997, 'The construction of women's management skills and the marginalisation of women in senior management', Women in Management Review, Vol.12, Issue 7.

The Economist (2005) Helping Women Get To The Top, July 23rd - 29th, Volume 376, Number 8436.

Thomas, P. T., 'Race Through The Planning Jungle' (1997), Recreation Management Journal, ISRM Published February (1998).

Thomas, P. T., And Meredith, T. (2002) 'Small Business Is Not A Little Big Business' Research Publication In The Effects Of Management Consultancy On SME's In South Wales. ISBA Conference 2001.

Thomas, R. and Pullen, A. (2000) 'Middle Management Identities in Modern Organisations', International Journal of Applied Management, 1, 1, pp.19-36.

Thomas, P. T., Talbot, L. And Mills, A. (2002) Entrepreneurs: An Ethnographic Study, British Academy Of Management, Refereed Paper, Conference 2002.

Thomas, P. T., Talbot, L. And Mills, A. 'Entrepreneurial Or Interapreneurial: The Case Of Asia, America & Europe' British Academy Of Management, Refereed Paper, Conference 2003.

Thomas, P. T., Talbot, L. And Williams, B. 'Innovation And Strategic Success; A Case Of Financial Services' British Academy Of Management, Refereed Paper, Conference 2002.

Thomas, P. T. And Xiou Xian (2003) 'Networking The Key To Success; Ethnographic Study' Conference Paper.

Thomas, P. T. And Whitehead, S. (2005) Female Entrepreneurs, Power, Leadership And Identity: A Chinese Perspective, Gender And Education Conference Cardiff University 2005, Full Paper.

Thomas, P. T. (2005) Gender Interpersonal Power, And Influence From A Complexity Thinking Perspective European Journal Of Complex Adaptive Systems Thinking, To Be Confirmed.

Thomas, J. (1993) Doing Critical Ethnography, Quality Give Research Methods Series 26, Sage University Paper, Sage Publications, London.
Tomlinson, A. (1995) Gender, Sport And Leisure; Continuities And Challenges. Chelsea Research Centre.

Tong, R.P. (1998) Feminist Thought; A More Comprehensive Introduction.(2nd Edn. Westview Press.

Triandis, H. C., M. D. Dunnette, & Hough, L. M. (1994). Handbook Of Industrial And Organizational Psychology. California: Consulting Psychology Press.

Tsang, J. (2002). The Grateful Disposition: A Conceptual And Empirical Topography. Journal Of Personality And Social Psychology, 82, 112-127.

Tsui, A. S., & Gutek, B. A. 1999. Demographic Differences In Organizations: Current Research And Future Directions. Lanham, MD: Lexington Books.

Tucker, S. (1990, July). What is the ideal body, Shape, pp. 94-112.

Turner, P. (1982) Academy Of Management Review, Jan2005, Vol. 30 Issue 1, P78, 18p.

## V

Van De Ven. (2000). Competing With New Product Technologies: A Process Model Of Strategy. Management Science. 46 (10) 1300-1316.

Ventor, K. (2002), Common Careers, Different Experiences: Women Managers In Hong Kong And Britain, Hong Kong University Press.

Vertinsky, P. (1995). Gender And The Physical Education Curriculum: The Dynamics Of Difference. In J. Gaskell & J. Willinsky (Eds.), Gender In/Forms Curriculum: From Enrichment To Transformation (Pp. 230-245). New York: Teachers College Press.

Vinnicombe, S. And Colwill, N. (1995) The Essence Of Women In Management. Prentice Hall.

Visweswaran, K. 1997. Histories of Feminist Ethnography. *Annual Review of Anthropology* 26, 591-621.

von der Lippe, G. (2002a). Media image: Sport, gender, and national identities in five European countries. International Review for the Sociology of Sport, 37, 371-395.

von der Lippe, G. (2002b). Medical texts on gender, sexuality, and sport in Norway, 1890-1950: Changing metaphors on femininities and masculinities. Journal of Sport History, 27, 481-495.

Vroom, V. H. `A New Look At Managerial Decision Making', Organizational Dynamics, 1(4) (1973), 66±80.

Veal A. J. And Ticehurst, G. W. (2000) Business Research Methods: A Managerial Approach, Longman, London.

**W**

Walby, S. (1997) Gender Transformations. Routledge.

Wang, P., (2000) Aching For Beauty: Foot Binding In China. Minneapolis: University Minnesota Press.

Ward, L. M. (2003). Understanding the role of entertainment media in the sexual socialization of American youth: A review of empirical research. Developmental Review, 23, 347-388.

Weber, M. (1947) The Theory Of Social And Economic Organisation, Oxford University Press, London.

Weedon, E. (1987) Conflict Management In US - Chinese Joint Ventures: An Analytical Framework, Management Issues In China, Volume 2, International Enterprises, Routledge, London.

Weick, K.E. And Roberts, K.H. (1993) 'Collective Mind In Organizations: Heedful Interrelating On Flight Decks' Administrative Science Quarterly, September.) Wengraf (2001).

Westwood, S. Hall-Taylor, B. And Chow, Y. (1997). "Writing Women Into Management Or Writing Ourselves Out: A Dilemma For Women As Authors." Women In Management Review, 12(8), 309-319.

Whitaker, K. S. (1998). Implementation Processes, Structures, And Barriers To High School Restructuring: A Case Study. Journal Of School Leadership, 8, 504-532.

Lightning Source UK Ltd.
Milton Keynes UK
UKOW07f1211140515

251517UK00007B/22/P